WELCOME TO THE REBELUTION

Seven Steps to the nutrition counseling practice of your dreams

KAIT FORTUNATO GREENBERG, RD, LD
REBECCA BITZER, CEO, MS, RD, CEDRD
DANA MAGEE, RD, LD

Welcome to the REBELution:
Seven Steps to the Nutrition Counseling Practice of Your Dreams
by Kait Fortunato Greenberg, Rebecca Bitzer, and Dana Magee

Books may be purchased by contacting the author at:
Rebecca Bitzer MS, RD & Associates
7219 D Hanover Parkway
Greenbelt, MD 20770
(301) 474-2499
admin@rbitzer.com

Cover & Interior Design: Summer Morris, Sumo Design Studio
Publisher: Empowered Enterprises
Editor: Dawn Josephson, Master Writing Coach
ISBN: 978-0-9904010-0-1
Printed in the United States of America

DEDICATION

To our clients. Working with you brings such joy and purpose into our lives. Thank you for sharing your stories and letting us be a part of your journey.

To our fellow REBEL Dietitians and students who inspire us daily.

To future nutrition students, dietetic interns, and Registered Dietitians, we hope to encourage you to follow your vision and the path that brings you happiness and fulfillment.

CONTENTS

ACKNOWLEDGEMENTS

We would like to thank the many people who offered assistance, inspiration, and support during the preparation and execution of this workbook.

Thank you to all our nutrition interns, both past and present, who continue to inspire us every day to do better. You definitely keep us on our toes with your desire to learn as much as you can from us as your mentors.

Thank you to our families who believed in us and supported us every step of the way. We are sure you had no idea how much time and energy we would put into this book and how much you would be involved in the process. We are very grateful for your support.

Thank you to all the REBEL-minded Registered Dietitians who came before us.

Thank you to Jessica Setnick, MS, RD, CEDRD for believing that our book will help start a REBELution and empower Registered Dietitians everywhere.

Thank you to our editor, Dawn Josephson, for helping us clarify our thoughts and ideas and for teaching us that it is really okay to end a sentence with a preposition.

Thank you to our cover designer, Summer Morris, who continued to work with us on our ever-changing ideas.

Thank you to each other for making this writing experience so memorable and fun. We each brought our strengths together to make this book so much more than it would have been if we had done it alone.

Kait, you have unbelievable focus, determination, and an endless ability to concentrate, which helped us get this book done in record time.

Dana, you have an incredible spirit and enthusiasm to keep us energized through the challenges of actually putting our thoughts and ideas into written words.

Rebecca, thank you for the entire basis on which this book was built. Without your passion, vision, determination, and years of experience in running Rebecca Bitzer & Associates, this book would not exist. Thank you for putting your time, energy, creativity, and financial backing into this book. It was amazing to feel your excitement for each and every page that was written. Your positivity fueled this process and made it an absolute joy. Thank you for bringing us REBELs together and believing in us from the time you brought us on as student volunteers to now. If even one ounce of your determination and innovation inspires our readers they will find an improvement in their work life and personal life.

INTRODUCTION

by Rebecca Bitzer, MS, RD, CEDRD
CEO of Rebecca Bitzer MS, RD & Associates (RBA)

REBEL Dietitian™ or Registered Dietitian (RD)? When you think about yourself and your career path, do you consider yourself a traditional Registered Dietitian or more of a REBEL Dietitian?

Typically, Registered Dietitians are very intellectual and scientifically trained to provide recommendations based on outcome studies. You have been trained to be nutrition experts; however, since the traditional path to becoming a Registered Dietitian involves so much technical training, chances are you didn't have much time in your academic years to become business savvy.

The authors of this book, Kait Fortunato Greenberg, Dana Magee, and I, are all Registered Dietitians in excellent standing with the Academy of Nutrition and Dietetics; however, we are on a mission to start a REBELution to empower Registered Dietitians to be REBEL Dietitians. We want to stir up the REBEL inside of you to help you design a career path that is more rewarding for you, both personally and professionally. Your career path today may be traditional, but you can choose to make it new and edgy. To do so, you need to search inward to discover the Registered Dietitian you were meant to be. Whether you are in private practice or want to travel down a personalized road to your dream, we want to help you clarify your values, set goals that match your values, and empower you to learn and practice new skills to create your own rich and meaningful career.

We believe that Registered Dietitians have traditionally been underpaid, often unspecialized, and historically misunderstood. As such, we have dedicated ourselves to boldly recreate our image, our profession, and our value. We have taken our incredibly powerful traditional

Registered Dietitian training and combined it with additional skills and calculated risks to become more REBEL-minded.

We realize that Registered Dietitians, even Registered Dietitians in non-traditional careers such as private practice, have been stuck in some outdated thinking patterns. We believe that instead of complaining about our career paths, we can be more rebellious, think outside of the traditional path, and create a personally and professionally fulfilling career.

We asked ourselves: Why couldn't more Registered Dietitians succeed in private practice? Why couldn't more Registered Dietitians finally earn what they're really worth? Why couldn't more Registered Dietitians hire employees? Why couldn't more Registered Dietitians have a career that's completely fulfilling and aligns with their values?

I would like to share with you my personal story to illustrate how you can be more REBEL-minded and how this workbook can walk you through the steps of creating your own successful private practice. Until now, I've never really thought of myself as a REBEL. But looking back, I was quite bold. I started my private practice when people told me that I could never earn a living that way. I created the Empowered Eating program and charged what it was worth when people told me I would never get clients to sign up. I started hiring a team of Registered Dietitians when people told me I could never have enough business to support them. I purchased an office suite when I was told by my previous landlord that I would fail.

I think my rebellion started with my first job as a Nutrition Analyst for the federal government. At the time, I did not realize that working for a large bureaucracy had very limited potential for advancement and would stifle my creativity. By nature, I need to express myself, be innovative, and consistently look for better and different ways to do things. Working for the federal government was not a good fit for my creativity and desire to connect with people and transform lives.

I started my private practice as a way to be in charge of my future and to be able to implement my ideas. Of course, I didn't jump in blindly. I may have been a REBEL, but I wasn't naive. I kept my full-time job with the federal government and started counseling clients and teaching classes in the evenings a few nights per week. Gradually, as I built my private practice, I changed my government hours to have every Friday off, and eventually I went to part-time. After eight months of consistent and hard work, I finally took the plunge and quit the stability of my government job (ultimately losing the safety net of my weekly paycheck). That was in 1989, and I haven't looked back since.

This is not to say it's been a smooth ride the entire time. I certainly have made some business gaffes over the years. Often, my career choice did not seem like a stable one, but because I love what I do and I can constantly learn and grow, I have built a successful business, Rebecca Bitzer MS, RD & Associates (RBA): The Nutrition Experts, using my talents.

Because I have rebelled from the traditional career path of Registered Dietitians and have learned from my missteps along the way, my business has soared. Today, I have unlimited earning potential and I am able to use my creativity on a daily basis. If you asked me whether I would do this all over again, my answer would be a resounding "YES." However, I would have loved to have had a workbook like this one to guide me and help me overcome obstacles. When I started my practice there were very few trailblazers at the time and only one guidebook on private practice for Registered Dietitians. Even today, there are only a few books for Registered Dietitians in private practice.

In addition to my personal rebellion, I seem to have attracted like minded REBELs in my business. My REBEL business team consists of Kait Fortunato Greenberg, RD and Dana Magee, RD. They both started working for RBA as student interns and worked their way up the corporate ladder. I have personally mentored Kait, and she in turn has mentored Dana. This mentor/mentee approach has worked incredibly well for us, and I hope it inspires you to do the same.

I am so passionate about what I have created that my mission is to share what I know with others, just like I have done with Kait and Dana. That's why the three of us strong-willed, rebellious Dietitians combined our strengths and passion to further our profession with this unconventional workbook so you can build your own successful private practice. We encourage you to utilize the activities and exercises in this book, as they are the exact steps I took that have strengthened my business throughout the years.

In this seven step workbook, you will learn some REBEL strategies to realize your potential, cultivate business skills, find your unique specialty, create a vision board, and set up accountability and support systems to foster your clients' and your business' success. We define these steps as REBEL RD:

R – Realize Your Potential
E – Excel in One Area of Dietetics
B – Build Your Private Practice
E – Empower Your Clients to Be Successful and Happy
L – Learn Ways to Keep Your Practice Financially Successful
R – Reach New Heights
D – Dare to Be a REBEL

In the remaining pages, Kait will share common private practice challenges as well as our REBEL Success Strategies with activities to help you conquer the roadblocks and guide you step-by-step to make your dreams a reality.

Welcome to the REBELution!

REBEL RD

CHAPTER ONE

R – Realize Your Potential

Create a Fulfilling Private Practice by Doing What You Love and Earning What You Deserve

What does RD mean to you? Registered Dietitian? REBEL Dietitian? Why not both? If you are reading this book, you are probably already a Registered Dietitian or you are well on your way to becoming one. So let's focus on how to stir up the REBEL in you so you can create your career path in private practice by doing what you love and earning what you deserve.

WHAT IS A REBEL DIETITIAN?

A REBEL Dietitian is one who has decided to break out of the traditional clinical Registered Dietitian career path. Don't get me wrong … being a clinical Registered Dietitian is a great career, but some Registered Dietitians are ready to hit the ground running in business and take an entrepreneurial spin on the field of nutrition and dietetics. Perhaps this describes you.

The field of dietetics is unbelievably exciting right now. I hope to inspire you to dive in to make your decision to be a Registered Dietitian one you will never regret. In this workbook, I encourage you to follow our Seven Steps to Achieving the Nutrition Practice of Your Dreams so you can ignite your passion in dietetics, develop skills you will need to thrive in private practice, and dare to REBEL to create your own success.

This workbook is designed to help you think beyond the traditional solo private practice and dream big to create a unique group practice that fosters long-term success, stability, and ultimately a legacy that will last for many years to come. Although there are undoubtedly several ways to make this happen, I am going to share with you how the REBEL team flourished. I want to show you how a private practice can bring you great joy and pride as you learn, grow, and create your own successful career. Not only do I want you to create a job that you love, but I also want to give you concrete information and tips from Rebecca, Dana, and I who have been "in the trenches." Our ultimate goal is to help you do what you love and give you the insight so you can earn what you deserve.

In this chapter you will do some introspective work to help you Realize Your Potential. To help you find or create a career that fits your personality, passion, and values, you will identify your strengths (using several tools such as the Myers-Briggs and StrengthsFinder), clarify your values (using mind tools and vision boards), and build on essential REBEL traits (positivity, gratitude, self-care, and giving back). I will help you foster these skills to create your unique vision.

FIND YOUR STRENGTHS

Before you even begin to think about a business model, take some time to sit and think about yourself. In order to excel in any career, and especially to grow your private practice, you must utilize your strengths and allow yourself to do what you do well. However, you must also accept the fact that others might do a better job at something than you will. Being able to distinguish these differences is a sign of a true leadership. In later chapters, I will help you decide when to do it yourself and when to bring in outside help. For now, let's focus on knowing and understanding your unique strengths, as that's key to realizing your potential.

Evaluate your strengths and those of your employees using these tools:

- **Essentials of Myers-Briggs Type Indicator Assessment (MBTI) (Essentials of Psychological Assessment) by Naomi L. Quenk, PhD**
  The MBTI, which you can find online, will classify your personality temperament, helping you to understand what energizes you, what qualities help you get projects completed, what situations help you thrive, how you make decisions, and how you work best with others. There is no one "best" type. All sixteen types have a variety of strengths. Knowing your type and the types of those with whom you interact will help you work together more efficiently and cooperatively. For example, if your biggest weakness is the ability to delegate, having a strong team of Registered Dietitians and administrative staff upon whom you can rely on to assign projects is vital for being able to delegate without fear. You can attempt to handle everything on your own, but it will leave you tired, unhappy, and vulnerable to burnout. By learning your own strengths and weaknesses, you can better delegate and take charge of your career without having to do everything yourself.

- **StrengthsFinder 2.0 by Tom Rath**
  This resource, which you can also find online, measures 34 strength themes, evaluated in the order in which you possess the traits from highest to lowest. It will also give you

an example of how each trait will impact your behaviors. Identifying your strengths will help you to plan and act on what you do best and what makes you happiest. By also taking note of your weaknesses, you can find ways to make those areas stronger and set goals to improve upon them. Of course, when in doubt, hire out. Don't be afraid to either hire a coach that can help you in your weaknesses or delegate those tasks outside of your business. At the end of the day you want a healthy and happy business and personal life, so do not dwell on your weaknesses; rather, use them as an opportunity to grow.

Focusing on your strengths is a great way to foster self-esteem and individuality. Creating a business based upon your strengths will keep you ahead of the pack, as natural strengths fueled by passion is not something that can be taught. Your strengths are unique to you, and focusing on them will enable you to realize your potential. When you utilize your strengths day in and day out and recognize where you need help, improving your skills your business will succeed. Remember to repeat this exercise several times over the course of your career as you build and develop new skills.

Inspiration from Rebecca: "Being detail-oriented is not one of my strengths. So instead of trying to force myself to do something that requires this skill, like bookkeeping or billing, it makes much more sense for me to hire a part-time bookkeeper or biller. By doing this, I can focus my time and energy on doing what I do well, using my strengths as a learner. I am drawn to the process of learning; however, I like to learn a lot on a new subject in a short time, and then move on to the next. The thought of doing something tedious like bookkeeping or billing is definitely not my cup of tea."

CLARIFY YOUR VALUES AND ALIGN THEM WITH YOUR STRENGTHS

When you visualize your ideal job, do you consider your values? Of course, everyone has a vague idea of what they value, but have you really dug deep to verbalize and take ownership of your values? Most people have not.

Values can simply include a list of 10 words that describe things that make you feel happy, proud, and fulfilled. Knowing who you are now and who you want to be will help you move closer to rebelliously doing what you love and earning what you deserve, or as we like to say, "Have your cake and eat it too!" This is how you achieve the reality of "if you love what you do you will never work a day in your life." That key piece of life advice has been stated by many, but the question is: HOW do you create a job where you LOVE to go to work every day? The answer is by matching your personal values to those of your business.

Inspiration from Dana: "You don't have to do something that doesn't fit your strengths and values just because that is a natural step. So many times I hear dietetic students, dietetic interns, and Registered Dietitians say, 'I want to do private practice, BUT I will start in the hospital first.' With our help, your drive, and passion you can start out doing what you love."

If you've never consciously thought about your values, that's okay. You're not alone. Here is a great tool to help you identify your values and passion, which will help to create your vision (more on vision in the next step).

WHAT ARE YOUR VALUES?

Review the following list of values (abbreviated from mindtools.com). Choose the three words that resonate most with you.

- ☐ Accuracy
- ☐ Achievement
- ☐ Adventurous
- ☐ Altruism
- ☐ Balance
- ☐ Being the Best
- ☐ Boldness
- ☐ Challenge
- ☐ Commitment
- ☐ Community
- ☐ Consistency
- ☐ Contentment
- ☐ Cooperation
- ☐ Courtesy
- ☐ Creativity
- ☐ Decisiveness
- ☐ Democraticness
- ☐ Dependability
- ☐ Determination
- ☐ Economy
- ☐ Effectiveness
- ☐ Efficiency
- ☐ Elegance
- ☐ Empathy
- ☐ Enjoyment
- ☐ Enthusiasm
- ☐ Excellence
- ☐ Expertise
- ☐ Family-Oriented
- ☐ Fitness
- ☐ Focus
- ☐ Freedom
- ☐ Fun
- ☐ Generosity
- ☐ Goodness
- ☐ Growth
- ☐ Happiness
- ☐ Hard Work
- ☐ Health
- ☐ Helping Society
- ☐ Honesty
- ☐ Honor
- ☐ Humility
- ☐ Improvement
- ☐ Independence
- ☐ Inner Harmony
- ☐ Inquisitiveness
- ☐ Intelligence
- ☐ Leadership
- ☐ Legacy
- ☐ Love
- ☐ Loyalty
- ☐ Making a Difference
- ☐ Mastery
- ☐ Merit
- ☐ Originality
- ☐ Positivity
- ☐ Practicality
- ☐ Preparedness
- ☐ Professionalism
- ☐ Reliability
- ☐ Resourcefulness
- ☐ Security
- ☐ Self-Actualization
- ☐ Serenity
- ☐ Speed
- ☐ Spontaneity
- ☐ Stability
- ☐ Strategic
- ☐ Strength
- ☐ Structure
- ☐ Success
- ☐ Support
- ☐ Teamwork
- ☐ Thankfulness
- ☐ Thoroughness
- ☐ Thoughtfulness
- ☐ Understanding
- ☐ Uniqueness
- ☐ Unity
- ☐ Vision

After you have determined your values, it is time to figure out a way to align them with your career in order to focus on your happiness and fulfillment, both personally and professionally.

For instance, if you place high value on independence, freedom, and flexibility, a 9 – 5 day job may leave you feeling trapped.

If you value making a difference, you will feel energized fostering your clients' growth.

If you value community and teamwork, you may find a group practice setting is just what you are searching for.

No matter what you value, if you are doing what you do best and living your values every day, you are a perfect fit for becoming a REBEL Dietitian!

Inspiration from Rebecca: "You are embarking on an exciting and challenging journey where you are likely to encounter obstacles along the way. I hope that this workbook will help you fine-tune your skills and your goals as you create a full and meaningful career of your own design."

FOUR REBEL TRAITS TO CULTIVATE

As REBEL Dietitians, we place immense value on positivity, gratitude, self-care, and giving back. The following section provides some insight on how we see these values being important in our business. Whatever values you have chosen, be sure you develop your thoughts on what those words mean to you. Don't just have words on paper. Find the meaning behind your words and values.

Positivity

The important thing to remember when growing a private practice is that you are going to make mistakes, feel overwhelmed, and be stressed. The best advice I can give is to stay positive. Everything happens for a reason, and when things are not going well (and this will happen) it is important to take a breath, examine the situation, and get help. Along the way, take time to appreciate where you are and all you have accomplished, learn from your mistakes and failures, and be kind to yourself and others.

The power of positive thinking goes a long way. Realize that your thoughts control your everyday life, so don't limit yourself with negative thinking. Every thought you have can either bring you closer to your values or cause you to drift away from them. Positive thoughts are the key to keeping true to your goals, your values, and yourself.

To enhance your ability to stay positive, write a list of self-empowering affirmations that resonate with you and say them out loud each morning to start your day off on the right foot.

Some examples are:

- I am a strong, powerful professional who is extremely successful and a born leader.
- I am a compassionate woman who deserves to enjoy life.
- I am always learning and growing; when I know better I will do better.

Gratitude

Most people are attracted to those who show appreciation versus those who rush through life and never seem satisfied. Showing gratitude helps you and those around you realize that good things are happening even when the situation may not seem ideal. This not only helps you keep a positive mindset, but it also sets a good example for your employees and clients.

Additionally, when your employees and clients feel valued, they are motivated to do their best—for you and themselves. Fostering an environment of gratitude helps your employees and clients feel like they are part of the team, which encourages and gives them the confidence to keep coming back and working hard.

Therefore, take action each week to practice gratitude by writing a thank you note to a client or employee, retweet or mention another colleague in your social media posts, or write in a gratitude journal. As the Hausa Proverb reminds us: "Give thanks for a little and you will find a lot."

Self-Care

Additionally, take care of yourself so you can be a positive role model for your team and your clients. To do so, schedule time each day for self-care to recharge and rest. Some ideas include:

- Turning off all electronics while eating lunch
- Taking a 15 minute walk outside between clients
- Going to a coffee shop to read fiction or inspirational novels
- Watching an inspirational YouTube video or TED Talk
- Getting a massage or pedicure at the end of the week
- Taking a bath at the end of a long day

Balancing a healthy lifestyle will positively impact your self-esteem, enhance the success of your business, and keep you from burning out. Take on a "work hard, play hard" mentality. You deserve it!

Giving Back

As you will read in later chapters, one of the pillars we stand on here at Rebecca Bitzer MS, RD & Associates (RBA): The Nutrition Experts is giving back to the field of dietetics by strengthening the young Registered Dietitians of tomorrow. We make it a priority to pay it forward and give our interns the opportunity to grow and learn outside of their university walls. This brings us great joy.

Here are some other examples of how you can give back in the nutrition community and your local community:

- Run for a position with the Academy of Nutrition and Dietetics or a favorite Dietetic Practice Group.
- Speak for charity at schools, community centers, or other groups.
- Give back to your niche such as National Eating Disorder Association (NEDA) or Step Out Diabetes walks and other ways of raising awareness.
- Start a Facebook campaign for donations to organizations near and dear to your heart.
- Volunteer at food drives, meals on wheels, or soup kitchens.
- Speak at colleges and universities about nutrition topics.

Kait Fortunato participating in Eating Disorder awareness events with the Eating Disorder Network of Maryland.

Rebecca Bitzer speaking to a sorority at the University of Maryland for Fat Talk Free Week.

Be sure to find a way for your business to give back that aligns with your values and niche.

SET YOUR VISION

You have identified your strengths and learned about essential traits to cultivate. Now it is time to set your vision and build a support system. Having a strong vision will bring you a profit and enable you to stay true to your values. Often, this step is challenging because you may be stuck in traditional thinking of what you "should" do. Here I hope to inspire you to get down to basics and think about things that you enjoyed when you were a child—in fact, something as simple as arts and crafts can help you tap into your creativity and think outside of the dietetics box. You are responsible for your own future so get out there and create the life you really want!

One fun and powerful exercise to help you develop your vision is to create a "vision board"—a collage of images that speak to you about your goals. Include personal or professional goals and/or a combination of both. (Remember, you are aligning both your personal and your business values to create your vision.) The idea is to have a visual reminder of what you want for your life and your business on paper to help you keep your focus and move you closer to your goals.

Dana Magee's REBEL vision board.

Your subconscious mind works on this image all the time whether you realize it or not, so you might as well give your subconscious mind specific, positive images to dwell upon. Take this vision board one step further and think of it as an action board. In other words, this board is making a promise to yourself for what you want to happen. The key is for you to set up ways to stay accountable to reach your vision (more on that later); otherwise, it will simply remain a vision.

Vision boards are especially helpful during times when you feel defeated or unsure of where you are going. Your vision board can help you keep in mind your passion and the big picture. As you share your inspiring images and goals with others, it helps you to move closer to these goals, because now you have outside accountability as well.

Inspiration from Dana: "I started working at RBA as a Registered Dietitian before I created my personal vision board. Interestingly, the values I represented on my board with magazine photos are direct parallels with my current position in the company. I have that board hung next to my desk as a constant reminder of what's important to me."

For more inspiration and accountability, visit our website at www.rbitzer.com.

Always remember that you can have great ideas and plans, but they are worthless if they always stay on your "to-do list" and are never put into action. Therefore, stay focused on what you want from your business and set short-term and long-term goals for your success. Next we'll discuss some tools and ideas to help you stay focused on achieving these goals.

ACCOUNTABILITY & GOAL-SETTING TOOLS

It's vital that you revisit your goals on a regular basis to stay positive and focused. At the beginning of the week, create a to-do list that includes work-oriented tasks and self-care. Keep track of what you accomplish on a "success log." This success log can be as simple as a journal or spreadsheet to keep your triumphs fresh in your mind as a way of celebrating all you have done. Items on this log may include books you have read, connections you have made, programs you have sold, and clients you have empowered.

If you find yourself stuck or having trouble staying focused on the path to your vision, connect with a trusted friend or mentor in order to help you stick to your goals and progress. Ask this person to help keep you accountable for what you want to achieve. When the two of you meet, use a template to evaluate your progress and stay true to your values, as the more accountable you are, the sooner you will achieve your vision. You can meet with this person weekly, monthly, or even quarterly. The important thing is to carve out time to meet and evaluate your progress.

Think of this accountability just like what you do with your clients. You know that your clients will progress more quickly if they meet with their Registered Dietitian more frequently;

the same is true with meeting with someone to stay accountable to your business vision and goals.

Here is a sample Goal-Setting Checklist you can use to stay on track:

Goal Setting Checklist Template: Fill this out prior to every accountability check-in.

1. What do you love about your career?
2. What would you like to be different about your career and how might this happen?
3. What are your top three personal values?
4. What are your top three professional values?
5. What have been your top three successes and challenges since our last meeting?
6. What are your goals for this month?
7. What are your goals for this week?
8. What will you do for fun/self-care?
9. What are you grateful for?
10. What will you accomplish before we meet again?

PROFESSIONAL BUSINESS COACHES

When you are really moving outside your comfort zone and feeling rebellious, hire a professional business coach who is skilled in helping you break through personal and professional barriers. Hiring a professional coach to guide your strengths and values based on your vision can help you stay accountable and reach your goals.

Our REBEL team has hired numerous Registered Dietitian coaches over the years who helped us keep the ball rolling and never stay comfortable. Consider this advice from Marjorie Geiser, Business Success Coach: "We live in our own stories of what we believe is possible for us. When we work with a coach … (we have) an objective advocate who can see our opportunities, strengths, and abilities that we often can't see in ourselves. By using a business coach, we are challenged to take the steps forward that we DREAM of, but often might hold back from, for any number of reasons."

PROFESSIONAL PEERS

There is no reason to go at this all alone, even in a solo private practice. Another strong source of growth can come from your dietetic and entrepreneurial peers. This field is unique in that we build each other up and the success of each individual strongly reflects the success of the profession. You will be so inspired by the individuals you meet and thankful for the friendships you will make.

Therefore, get involved in the nutrition community. This will help you to gain knowledge, credibility, and expertise in your area of dietetics and nutrition private practice. But simply signing up for the e-mail lists is not enough; make sure your voice is heard by actively participating in the group discussions. Get involved with the executive board to network with other Registered Dietitians in your field. Don't be afraid to start small. The most important thing is to get out there and start connecting to other professionals. My recommendations include:

- **Nutrition Entrepreneurs (NE):** This is a Dietetic Practice Group (DPG) for Registered Dietitians in business. Their vision is "shaping the future of dietetics by pursuing innovative and creative ways of providing nutrition products and services to consumers, industry, media, and business." Find out more about this group at www.nedpg.org. In this group you will come in contact with REBEL Dietitians who break out of the typical Registered Dietitian mold and provide tips on how to become a local and national celebrity in your field. NE is where we met our business coach, mastermind group (we will discuss this later), and writing coach, and it will be your go-to resource when seeking inspiration and information.
- **Local/State Dietetic Practice Group:** Being an active member of your local group will help increase publicity of your practice and specialty. You will receive various referrals from Registered Dietitians in your area who are looking for someone whom they can trust with your specific skill set. You will be awarded speaking opportunities, made aware of nutrition related events, and be asked for quotes in local publications. It's free advertising at its finest.
- **Mastermind Groups:** Reach out to Registered Dietitians in other communities to create a professional support system that can be based on specialties (eating disorder, digestive, etc.) on a particular field of dietetics (private practice, authors, etc.) or a connection of professionals outside of dietetics. In these groups you can gain other points of view and have accountability and support outside of the people you work with on a daily basis. They will provide inspiration and honest feedback.

Inspiration from Rebecca: "One of the most amazing things I have done is be accountable to my mastermind group. For one hour each week, I collaborate with two other Registered Dietitians to help me challenge myself to grow and follow through with my vision. I also empower my two REBEL Dietitians in the same way."

- **Professional Events:** Attending professional conferences and nutrition-related community events helps you stay current and is a great way to be recognized as the expert. Clients will respect the love you have for continued growth and learning, and you will leave these conferences full of energy and ideas. Stay current with events being advertised by subscribing to professional newsletters and blogs that may send out information regarding upcoming events. Heavily weigh what you will be getting out of the specific event or conference. Here are some things to think about:
    - How much value will you get out of the conference?
    - What are the fees to sign up or attend?
    - Will the travel time to the event be unreasonable since you cannot be counseling clients during this time?
    - Will you offer reimbursement for these conferences to your staff as a perk?
    - What's the point of attending the event? Will it bring referrals to your door? Tools for your counseling? More expertise? Networking for your advancement in your career?
    - What sessions are being offered that will positively impact your practice?

When you attend, be sure to leave each event with one or more take-away items. These can be tangible or intangible things, such as:

- New goals you will hold yourself accountable to
- New contacts to follow up with
- Ideas for blogs that you can share on your social media profiles and use in your newsletters (more on this later)
- Notes to share with your staff to further their learning

- Photographs of you with various speakers at the event to share on your social media profiles. This will help to commemorate your meeting so they will remember you in the future and increase your reach. It will also show gratitude for the speaker. For example, I attended a Fancy Food Show in Washington DC and had the pleasure of meeting Food Network Chef Emeril Lagasse. He shared his respect for our work as Registered Dietitians and agreed to take a photo with me, which I immediately blogged about and received various comments and "likes."

Stay consistent with the conferences you attend. Each year you can continue to build relationships, network with familiar faces, and stay current. Our REBEL team prioritizes conferences such as the Food and Nutrition Conference and Expo (FNCE); the Sports, Cardiovascular and Wellness Nutrition's (SCAN) Annual Meeting (following the disordered eating and eating disorders track); the Binge Eating Disorder Association (BEDA) Conference; the Academy of Eating Disorders; the National Association of Eating Disorders; and various treatment centers' continuing education programs. Make it a goal to contact and stay in touch with physicians that can work with you and clients in your specialty. Knowing the people involved with each treatment center, seeing the location, and studying the mission helps you match your clients with the best fit possible.

Inspiration from Rebecca: "It is definitely worth your time and energy to volunteer for any professional organizations that you are passionate about. By volunteering you will meet amazing like-minded professionals, and these groups may even help out with your fees. As mentor coordinator for Nutrition Entrepreneurs, I made life-long friends and business associates and never had to pay for travel to amazing conferences and board meetings."

- **Your Local Community:** Think of every experience as a way to market yourself and your business. Examples of places where you can become known include church groups, synagogues, rotary clubs, Girl Scouts, and school Parent Teacher Associations (PTA). Becoming active in these groups is a nice way to give back to the community and also increase awareness of your profession.

Never stop looking for things to inspire you and sharpen your skills. You will thrive from regularly reviewing blogs, videos, podcasts, books, and workbooks for inspiration, business success, and advances in evidenced-based practice. There are so many valuable resources that it is easy to get overwhelmed. Take advantage of the ever-growing and improving technology to keep you organized and connected, such as:

- Feedly and Flipboard to keep abreast of informational and inspirational blogs
- Google Drive to keep a list of compelling quotes and video links organized by topic
- Google Alerts and Smartbriefs for Nutritionists for automatic access to the top nutrition trends in your field
- Shared drive and hidden web pages to form a network for saving all handouts and resources

For some of our favorite resources, visit our website at www.rbitzer.com.

PROFESSIONAL ADVISORS

To align your goals and execute your vision safely and securely you must meet with the appropriate business professionals. By not asking the right specialist for business advice, it is akin to having your clients ask a fitness professional for nutrition counseling. While the fitness professional may know a little about nutrition, they aren't trained in nutrition and may inadvertently give inaccurate information. Similarly, if you ask your tax advisor for legal advice, you may end up in hot water.

I recommend you meet with the following individuals to ensure you are legally and financially prepared to have a successful business for many years to come:

- Lawyer to advise on the best way to structure and organize your business (LLC, s-corp, sole proprietorship, etc.)
- Banking professional to set up a business checking account and credit card used for all business transactions, separate from your personal accounts
- Financial advisor to set up retirement accounts and investments
- Tax advisor who will be able to prepare your business tax return
- In-house or outside billing personnel to work with insurance claims, perform collections, and handle billing statements (more on this later)
- Accountant/Bookkeeper to help create and manage your budget

- Legalzoom.com or some similar service to acquire a trademark for your program or business name
- Payroll service to automate the payroll process such as Paychex or the Intuit Payroll Suite available through many major banks

This list of professionals is by no means all inclusive. As you embark on the journey of private practice, seek out those professionals who can answer any questions you may have. Never just "wing it" and don't waste time trying to figure everything out on your own. Use other people's expertise and advice to shave years off your learning curve. And though you are spending money in the beginning, you will save money in the long run by getting the answers you need without costly mistakes.

IT'S YOUR BUSINESS - CREATE IT!

It is important that your business brings you closer to living a full, meaningful life. In order to achieve this, you must first realize your full potential by learning more about yourself, what is most important to you, and your core values that drive you. Remember, everything you are doing in life and business should draw you closer to your values, as that's the best way to reach your potential. But you can't do it alone! Reach out for help, inspiration, and encouragement so you can keep setting the bar high! The more you believe in what you are achieving, the more you will prosper.

REBEL SUCCESS STRATEGIES

ASSIGNMENTS:

☐ Take the Myers-Briggs Type Indicator Assessment and analyze your results with a description of each trait you possess.

What are your top five strengths?

____

____

____

____

____

How can you best utilize each strength?

What are your top five weaknesses?

How might these hold you back from achieving your vision?

Will you need to hire someone to help you overcome these weaknesses?

How will you work on your weaknesses?

☐ Create a vision board.

☐ Fill out the Goal-Setting Checklist Template:

1. What do you love about your career?

2. What would you like to be different about your career and how might this happen?

3. What are your top three personal values?

4. What are your top three professional values?

5. What have been your top three successes and challenges?

6. What are your goals for this month?

7. What are your goals for this week?

8. What will you do for fun/self-care?

____

____

____

____

____

____

9. What are you grateful for?

____

____

____

____

____

10. What will you accomplish before we meet again?

____

____

____

____

____

- For questions 3 and 4, do your values align? If not, what needs to be changed?

  ____

  ____

  ____

- For your challenges in question 5, how can you overcome these by setting goals in questions 6 and 7?

- Do you need to hire a coach or have a colleague hold you accountable?

☐ Set up your professional support network.

- Contact Registered Dietitians personally or via e-mail lists to start a mastermind group.
- Join Nutrition Entrepreneurs Dietetic Practice Group (DPG).
- Join your local Academy of Nutrition and Dietetics (A.N.D.) group.
- Join 2 Dietetic Practice Groups (DPG) that are relevant to your practice.

☐ Make and organize a list of professional development resources that you will use regularly. Start building your library full of inspirational, business, and nutrition books.

"You are only limited by your own imagination."

– Benny Bellamacina,
songwriter/musician, poetic humorist, and children's author

REBEL RD

CHAPTER TWO

E – Excel in One Area of Dietetics

Where Do You Want to Put Your Energy?

During my first few months as a Registered Dietitian, I had terrible anxiety and butterflies in my stomach the night before I was scheduled to meet with a client who did not fit my passion or specialty. I knew I was making a difference and helping people, but I was doing the client and myself a disservice by working within an area that did not truly energize me. It was not until I learned to say "no" to opportunities and really dive into my specialty that I could honestly say that I loved my work.

At this point, most people are thinking something like, "I can't turn away business! I need all the clients I can get." I understand that thinking, but realize that when you focus your energy on one specialty, both you and your clients win. For example, meet "Karen" (not her real name). She came into my office looking to practice mindful eating and develop a healthy relationship with food (my favorite type of work). After working together for a few weeks we also started to explore some food sensitivities and gastrointestinal pain she was having. Once these issues arose, I quickly referred her to a digestive Registered Dietitian. Karen was so grateful to me for not pretending to know what I did not, and the digestive Registered Dietitian helped her immensely. Today, Karen is one of my long-term clients and she often checks in with the digestive Registered Dietitian I referred her to. Another perk is that this digestive Registered Dietitian sends me her clients whenever they are looking to work on weight loss or intuitive eating. This is a win-win for everyone and a great example of how building your professional referral network is so helpful.

CLIENTS ARE THE HEART OF YOUR PRACTICE

By serving others as a Registered Dietitian you are making a lasting effect on them and transforming lives. You owe it to your clients and to yourself to deliver high-quality information and produce results. You are helping your clients reach their ultimate goals and you need to convey your passion confidently by working with clients who energize you and to whom you can relate.

It is even more important now than ever that Registered Dietitians are seeing clients who are a good fit. Why? Because nutrition information is everywhere—in magazines, online, posted on Facebook, on food labels … you name it. You must show your value by providing even better evidenced-based nutrition facts with a compassionate emphasis. This will individualize your recommendations much more than any handout, book, or article could ever do. Therefore, as a private practice Registered Dietitian, you need to develop areas of expertise to grow your practice with successful clients so you can deliver exceptional results and provide a peace of mind in your personal life. This will strengthen both our profession and your business.

By having a distinct specialty, when potential clients call your office they can confidently choose you knowing that your practice is the best fit for the job and that they will see results. If you are not best suited to meet the client's needs, you can cross-refer with other Registered Dietitians in your area (local affiliates) until you are able to hire Registered Dietitians of other specialties to eventually work for you. For example, I refer out for children under two years of age.

FIND THE CLIENTS THAT ENERGIZE YOU

To determine which clients you can best serve, begin by taking a look at yourself to determine where your nutrition and personal priorities align. You may find that your ideal clients are very similar to you. For example, consider …

- The Registered Dietitian who focuses on sports nutrition and who actively runs marathons and helps athletes fuel their performance.
- The Registered Dietitian who focuses on pediatric nutrition and who has a family and helps parents create a healthy relationship with food for their children.
- The Registered Dietitian who focuses on Binge Eating Disorder and emotional eating and who helps others REBEL against diets.

Now turn this to yourself. What do you typically like to read or do during downtime?

- Reading blogs about self care?
- Browsing cookbooks and finding new recipes?
- Going to farmer's markets?
- Traveling around the country?
- Bringing your kids into the kitchen?
- Gardening in your backyard?

Inspiration from Dana: "In my free time I love to cook for my family and friends and try new quick recipes. Since I am making these dishes anyway, I have started creating step-by-step food preparation cooking albums on my Facebook business page. This helps my clients by offering them ideas for healthy, quick meals and also lets them see how and what I am eating, including pizza!"

Once you have some ideas about your own likes and passions, determine how you can align what you already love to do and turn it into a successful business. You will get joy out of solving client issues that you relate to and working with people who energize you. Additional benefits to you include:

- You will get to do more of what you love whether it be cooking, sports, or meditation/relaxation.
- You will get to counsel, speak, and write about the topics that interest you.
- You will learn more about your specialty by seeing more of these clients and learning from them.
- You will be able to focus your energy on conferences, books, and collaboration with other specialists in your area (i.e. visiting treatment centers).
- You will have a chance to refer out to other Registered Dietitians and/or hire a Registered Dietitian that can provide expertise outside of your niche (more on this later).

But of course, it's not all about YOU. By having a distinct niche, your clients will also benefit. For example, consider these client-focused benefits:

- The client will feel your energy and your expertise.
- Your VIP clients will want the best of what you have to offer and will feel excited knowing they are getting star treatment.
- Your clients will be successful because you know the ins and outs of what they are going through.
- You know the right questions to ask in order to help your clients see results.
- You are the most up-to-date on the research and counseling methods for the issues they are struggling with.
- You will be inspired to write blogs and post on social media, which will continue to attract these clients and provide further support (more on this later).
- You will become the nutrition expert amongst health professionals in this field.

CREATE A PROGRAM THAT WILL APPEAL TO YOUR IDEAL CLIENT AND GROW YOUR PRACTICE

You now have your ideal clients and feel strongly about helping them see results. What is the next step? Here is where you have to be bold and take risks to break free from traditional insurance-based clientele to really make a difference in your clients' care and your income.

As of this writing, insurance only covers for face-to-face nutrition counseling. But what if your clients need more daily feedback? How can you give your clients more support and more services than insurance covers? Our REBEL approach helps you move away from solely appointment-to-appointment intervention so you can give people the tools and assistance they need to make a meaningful change in their life.

To answer the questions posed, think about how you can repackage all the services you currently provide and add in the specific tools for your clients' unique nutrition situation. This is called creating a program. Having a program (or programs to choose from) allows you to include new services so your clients don't have to purchase them à la carte, which may discourage them from investing in tools that would further their success. One way to think of a program is as "full service coaching" from start to finish.

When trying to explain a "program" to Registered Dietitians, the best analogy I can think of is getting braces for your teeth. If you've ever had braces or a child with braces, you know that the orthodontist does not charge you individually for each appointment, each wire that is adjusted, or each tooth that is straightened. Instead, the orthodontist charges you a flat fee to "straighten your teeth." Your orthodontist might even throw in a free tooth whitening session at the completion of your intervention. This is similar to how you should work your nutrition counseling program.

Sometimes the orthodontist might have additional skills or training that is not used; other times, you might require every single skill the orthodontist has. Either way, you are in it for the long haul—until you have the results you want. In other words, once you pay for the braces, you are all in. You are not going to stop after four appointments because you get too busy or distracted to continue. That is what the REBEL team aims to do with our clients. It is important to get clients focused on the whole program, on achieving the results that they want, and not make it easy for them to give up and quit. You want happy, healthy clients just as an orthodontist wants to help his clients achieve a great smile. Often, people pay out-of-pocket for straight teeth, so why would they not pay to solve their food and nutrition issues that they have been struggling with for a significant period of their lives?

Setting up programs is how our team evolved from the limitations of one-on-one counseling. By developing programs that offer a wide array of services you can help your clients get freedom from food struggles. Here is how you can set up a similar program. While the program you develop will be based on your unique specialty and training, we hope our example inspires you to do something creative to help your clients get results.

Rebecca Bitzer and Associate's first program, Empowered Eating, was designed for clients struggling with anorexia and bulimia, as well as their loved ones who were also suffering as a result of the disease. This program is primarily for people who want and need an intense program for their recovery while still attending work/school and living at home rather than going to a treatment center. It is also for people coming out of a treatment center who need additional support to help protect their recovery process while they transition back to their routine life.

Inspiration from Rebecca: "I will never forget the intense joy and excitement of launching my first program, Empowered Eating. With the help of my business coach, I was able to get off the 'work treadmill' of seeing client after client, take a step back to set my vision, and take action. Launching this program enabled me to be less stressed, more focused, and more fulfilled, and I was able to empower more successful clients. Two years later, I empowered my REBEL Dietitians to start their first program."

Inspiration from Dana: "I came to RBA at a very exciting time. I was energized by the success of Rebecca launching Empowered Eating and I was able to see it grow before my eyes. Little did I know that I would have the opportunity to follow in her footsteps to create the REBEL dieting program for clients that I felt passionate about—this time with her experience as a template."

Here are some tips on why the Empowered Eating program has become so successful. I also included a few things for you to think about when creating your first program:

- The first step to creating a successful program is to outline specific problems your ideal clients struggle with daily. Develop a questionnaire that your clients can fill out prior to coming into your first session that outlines problem areas and what they hope to achieve from working with you. This will help them identify how much pain they are truly in and how much they need your help and expertise. Here are some examples of questions to ask to help clients understand how much they are struggling:
    - *How is your struggle with food and weight impacting relationships with your family?*
    - *If all your energy was not put into food, what else could you accomplish?*
    - *Where do you see yourself six months from now and what can prevent you from getting there?*
- Next, detail what impact these challenges are having on your clients' lives.
    - *For example, when clients come to us initially, we often find that they avoid going out to eat with friends, restrict the foods they love, and have food-related thoughts consuming their everyday life.*
- Determine the results your clients will expect from participating in your program.
    - *We help clients effectively end destructive behavioral cycles and restore healthy habits, eat mindfully, empower themselves, and live joyfully.*
- Organize sound resources and evidenced-based protocols for your specialty program.
- Develop handouts and protocols based on the research regarding your clientele.
    - *For samples of our handouts, please visit our website at www.rbitzer.com.*

- Develop a plan. Consider such thing as how many sessions and for how long. Will you meet weekly or every other week?
    - *Treating clients with eating disorders means it is important to see them every week.*
- Determine if you will have one main program or different levels of care.
    - *The Empowered Eating program has different levels of treatment. After a client completes the initial program, we give them the option to renew or progress to the next phase of the program after meeting certain milestones.*
    - *This allows them to be a long-term client and provides tools and strategies for success.*
- Develop other forms of support for your clients such as a weekly or monthly support group, daily food log communication, or text and email support. This is one way to make your program unique.
    - *Utilize specialty smart phone applications for daily food log communication, such as Recovery Record.*
    - *Coordinate care with the other health professionals on the team, provide family support, and eat with clients.*
    - *Offer a free support group every week that is open to anyone as a way to give back to the community and attract others who may be struggling.*
    - *Take your program outside the office. For example, eat with your clients, conduct pantry makeovers, and shop the grocery store with them.*
    - *Send clients Nutrition Preparation forms to fill out before each visit for accountability purposes. This form should include what they have worked on since their last appointment and encourage them to reflect on their achievements and challenges to highlight areas to focus on next. This holds the client responsible and gives structure to the session.*
- Create a name for your program. Do you need a separate website, Facebook, or Twitter account for this program?
    - *The Empowered Eating program has a separate website, blog, Facebook page, and Twitter account.*
- Create a launch date for your program and stick to it.
    - *Do not let your perfectionism get in the way and hold you back from launching; you will continue to learn along the way.*

    - *"Internal research by Hewlett-Packard found that women only apply for jobs for which they feel they are a 100% match; men do so even when they meet no more than 60% of the requirements." –Sheryl Sandberg*

- Determine the fee for your program. Before you simply state a number, consider all the following factors:
    - *The number of appointments and the length of each visit.*
    - *Your level of expertise, certification, and credentials.*
    - *All the behind-the-scenes work you will be doing outside of face-to-face appointments. This includes coordinating care, reviewing food logs, phone calls with the family, running support groups, and additional workshops and training.*
    - *If you offer a payment plan for clients who may want to split payment in two or more payments, be sure you charge interest as an incentive to have clients pay all at once.*
    - *Don't offer discounts. List your fees and what's included in writing.*
    - **Do not be afraid to charge what you are worth.**
- Does your program take insurance?
    - *Our program does not take any insurance. Not only is insurance reimbursement low (more on this later), but self-pay programs help to protect the relationship with clients. We have had circumstances where insurance will not pay or even has taken money back and it is hard to talk "business" with clients when you are working on building trust with their eating disorders. By having clients invest in their health and commit to a program, they are more successful with treatment.*

Remember: If you trust in your program, have incorporated your personal and professional values, and continue to stay abreast of advances in nutrition, it will make counseling your clients and selling your program even easier because *you* will truly believe in its value. We work with our clients to get them any available out-of-network coverage for their visits by providing them with receipts so they can be reimbursed by their insurance company.

REBEL SUCCESS STRATEGIES

ASSIGNMENTS:

Answer these questions to create your ideal program:

- [ ] What specific problems are your ideal clients having that affect their day-to-day life?

___

___

___

- [ ] What questions can you ask new clients that outline their struggles the problem areas and what they hope to achieve from working with you?

___

___

___

___

- [ ] What impact are these challenges having on your clients' lives?

___

___

___

___

- [ ] What will your program include that will help these clients overcome these challenges?

___

___

___

___

- [ ] What resources and evidenced-based protocols do you need for your specialty program?

- [ ] How many sessions will you offer? Will you meet weekly or every other week?

- [ ] What behind-the-scenes work will you need to do in your program?

- [ ] Will you have more than one program or different levels of care?

- [ ] What other forms of support will you offer your clients?

- [ ] What will you name your program?

☐ Will you create a separate website for your program or add it to your existing website?

☐ Will you set up a Facebook or Twitter account for this program?

☐ What will be the launch date for your program?

☐ What will be the fee for your program?

☐ Will your program take insurance?

"There's a difference between interest and commitment. When you're interested in doing something, you do it only when it's convenient. When you're committed to something, you accept no excuses, only results."

– Unknown

CHAPTER THREE

B – Build Your Private Practice

Hiring Employees and Expanding Locations

If you love what you do and you are good at counseling, you will soon find that you don't have enough hours in the day to get everything done. When this happens, it's time to take the next step into transforming your solo private practice to a group practice. You may have had a variety of experiences consulting with web designers, accountants, or other for-hire professionals, which is a good start, but hiring your first employee adds an entirely new layer of sophistication.

Your time as a Registered Dietitian is very valuable. As a nutrition entrepreneur, you need to be conscious of your income earning time, because you can only see a limited number of clients each day, which is a natural shortcoming of being in private practice. You have an even smaller window of opportunity to see clients if you consider the amount of time you will need to spend on administrative tasks, such as bookkeeping, marketing, or even just cleaning the office. You could bring on more people to help you administratively, more people to help you counsel**, or both to be most efficient.**

WHEN IS IT TIME TO HIRE YOUR FIRST ADMINISTRATIVE STAFF MEMBER OR REGISTERED DIETITIAN?

Administrative Staff Member:

When you are really busy and working what feels like 24/7, and when you are spending your evenings doing billing, returning phone calls, writing notes, and researching information, it is time to hire someone to help you. You simply cannot continue at that pace without it taking a toll on your health or personal life.

Think of it like this: Does it make sense for you to routinely answer phones and drive to the post office, or is it better if you spend your time generating revenue while seeing clients? One way to help you identify if you need to make a new hire is to conduct a time study to keep track of how much time and energy you spend on certain tasks. If you discover that you spend over 10 hours a week on administrative tasks, it's time to hire your first administrative team member.

Registered Dietitians:

When you are getting too many referrals/clients to see, or if you are being contacted by clients outside of your niche, it may be time to hire another Registered Dietitian. For example, if you work mainly with those suffering from diabetes, and a gastroenterologist moves in next door and inquires about working together, you might consider hiring a Registered Dietitian who is passionate about digestive issues to fill this need.

Of course, it is difficult to predict when to hire another Registered Dietitian, because if you hire too early, then you will struggle with cash flow. There is nothing worse than paying another Registered Dietitian when you no longer have enough money to pay yourself what your time is worth. You are the business owner who took all the financial risk and life energy to get this business started; therefore, you want to be wise with your hiring.

So before you rush out and post a "help wanted" ad for a Registered Dietitian, consider both the benefits and challenges of bringing on this new person.

Benefits of hiring a new Registered Dietitian:

- The ability to profit from your Registered Dietitian's revenue stream.
- The opportunity to hire a Registered Dietitian with a specialty that is outside your nutrition niche (more on this later).
- Someone to cover for you if you are sick, on vacation, or on maternity/medical leave.
- A sense of community in what could be a lonely field of dietetics.
- An office of energized people to collaborate and problem solve with.
- The ability to discuss case studies in order to get new ideas.
- Ultimately creating a professional legacy, as your Registered Dietitians may one day run the practice that you created.

Inspiration from Dana: "Coming into the practice directly out of my internship, my experience could never compare to the hands-on experience from the years of counseling that Rebecca and Kait have. It is a true gift to be able to be mentored by both of these outstanding Registered Dietitians and have my questions, concerns, and ideas answered and evaluated right away. This benefits my personal growth as well as makes sure my clients receive the best care."

CHALLENGES OF HIRING A NEW REGISTERED DIETITIAN:

- If a client is not happy with the services your Registered Dietitian provides, it becomes your problem and a reflection of your practice as a whole.
- There are short-term costs with a new hire as you train them to build their practice.
- It is important to realize the "hidden" costs of employees. Some of them may include:
  - Payroll expenses (payroll taxes, workers compensation, social security)
  - Health insurance
  - Employee benefits (401K retirement accounts, health savings accounts, mileage reimbursement, phone reimbursement, vacation leave)
  - Electronic health records (fee for each provider)
  - Tablets, iPads, or additional equipment needed for each employee
  - Professional development for each employee
  - Reference materials
  - Professional liability expenses for each employee
  - Uniforms for each employee (if applicable)
  - Promotional materials for all nutrition counseling, events, and classes
  - Automobile expenses
  - Employee appreciation (bonuses, parties, team building events, mentoring)
  - Meals and entertainment
  - Travel
  - Dues and Dietetic Practice Group subscriptions

- Your advertising and promotion expenses will rise with each new Registered Dietitian you bring on, including:
  - Website (website design, hosting, maintenance, social media)
  - Referral listing websites
  - Brochures for each program
  - Business cards for each employee
- If you expand your office locations to accommodate more employees, your office upkeep expenses may rise too, such as:
  - Rent/mortgage (if you need a larger office space with the new employees)
  - Utilities (electricity)
  - Repair/maintenance
  - Internet
  - Telephone
  - Furniture
  - Office equipment (computers, iPads, tablets, furniture, scales, resting metabolic rate machines, body fat analysis, blood pressure cuffs)
  - Office supplies
  - Postage and delivery
  - Cleaning service
  - Shredding company
- Business expenses that could rise include:
  - Bank service charges (depositing more checks may increase your fees)
  - Credit card expenses
  - Business licenses and permits (you'll need a permit or license for each location)
  - Professional fees (accounting, bookkeeping, tax advising)
  - Clerical Staff
  - Taxes
  - Depreciation expenses

In chapter 5 we'll go into detail on how to track these and other expenses.

CONSIDERATIONS FOR HIRING REGISTERED DIETITIANS

In order to hire and retain great people, you need to conduct a successful interview. Here are some points of what to look for when hiring specifically in private practice:

- Business savvy and drive. Private practice Registered Dietitians cannot just be interested in counseling; they have to be involved in the business side of things in order to succeed.

Inspiration from Dana: "Since I was a new Registered Dietitian fresh out of my internship, you would think that other seasoned Registered Dietitians would beat me out when Rebecca decided to bring on another Registered Dietitian. However, after working for her as a student and showing great interest in the business aspect of RBA, I became an outstanding and sought after recruit. Ever since, members of RBA have interviewed numerous interested Registered Dietitians and once they state they are interested only in the counseling aspect with no mention of how they will be generating revenue, that's a red flag that this position may not be a good fit for them. You can be the best clinical Registered Dietitian out there, but without a way to keep your eye on the pulse of the business, you will not have a business to work for."

- All employees should have knowledge of the latest nutrition trends, technology, and communication. The person should have experience in blogging, website design, social media, and electronic health records (EHR).
- All employees must convey passion and warmth, be adept at building relationships with clients, and be flexible and adaptable in a fast-paced environment.
- All employees should also be open to change, especially in terms of new office policies and procedures and advancements in technology.
- Finally, you want employees who are organized and timely—who can get back with physicians, clients, and each other regarding client information.

The ideal person should come to the interview prepared with background information on your practice and should ask the right questions to align with your vision. This shows that they can "see" themselves in your practice, which is just as important as you being able to envision them working with you. It should be apparent that their personal values align with your company values.

Also, do not hire people over the phone. One interview is okay, but make sure to meet the candidate in person prior to hiring to see their energy level and body language.

Above all else, don't underestimate the importance of trusting your gut. If something doesn't feel right about the person, listen to that little voice in your head that's warning you. Remember, this person will be a reflection of you and your company.

MISTAKES TO AVOID WHEN HIRING REGISTERED DIETITIANS:

- Hiring when you're desperate, tired, or overstressed.
- Hiring without a non-compete agreement. A non-compete protects your business from an employee taking your clients, policies, and procedures and setting up shop in your area in direct competition.
- Being naive and believing that most people want to work as hard and as passionately as you do.
- Hiring people who are not detail-oriented and efficient.
- Bringing someone in as an independent contractor who should have been hired as an employee.

HOW TO HIRE: CONTRACTOR VS. EMPLOYEE

You may be tempted to utilize part-timers as independent contractors instead of hiring employees because it is easier and less expensive, but you must meet the strict criteria of the Internal Revenue Service (IRS) or severe penalties will occur. Based on our experience, it is nearly impossible to hire a Registered Dietitian as an independent contractor for your practice. If you are monitoring their work, assigning their schedule, and providing business cards and other office equipment, the IRS will consider these people to be employees.

Contact an attorney to make sure you are hiring correctly. Otherwise, if you classify your new hire incorrectly, you may be subject to high penalties and fees. For example, if you hired someone as an independent contractor who you later laid off, and if this person then applies for unemployment, you will be subject to penalty fees if the IRS deems this person should have been an employee. See this resource for more information: http://www.irs.gov/Businesses/Small-Businesses-&-Self-Employed/Independent-Contractor-Self-Employed-or-Employee.

Inspiration from Rebecca: "You may be tempted to be rebellious at this stage by doing it all yourself, but it is much wiser to listen to the experts and do it correctly the first time. Asking for professional help at this stage can save you time, money, and aggravation. As a business owner, you don't want to spend a sleepless night worrying about a mistake that could have been avoided. Understanding cash flow as well as corporate and payroll taxes took me hours of professional advice to master and understand the concepts."

HOW TO PAY REGISTERED DIETITIANS

People always ask about the correct way to pay employees. Unfortunately, it's a difficult question to answer. Rebecca has tried various ways to compensate employees and has found one system that works best for RBA. One way to get an idea of what to pay your Registered Dietitians is to look at the Academy of Nutrition and Dietetics (AND) compensation study on their website and plug in the appropriate numbers (http://www.eatright.org/salarycalculator/). Keep in mind that if you type in "private practice," your results will be much higher than if you type in "outpatient Registered Dietitian," which is more appropriate. Your employee will be more of an outpatient Registered Dietitian than a business owner and should be paid accordingly. You can also include the state in which you are working, your Registered Dietitian's credentials, years of experience, and education for the most accurate estimate.

Remember how long it took you to build up your practice? Although you are fast-tracking your new Registered Dietitian, this person will not be up and running overnight with a thriving client list. It may take six months to two years before she is booked solid. So think about whether you are going to pay your Registered Dietitian for time spent without clients while she is building her practice. If you overpay your employee and she is not bringing in revenue, you are going to incur significant expenses. However, if you don't compensate your Registered Dietitian for this time, you are going to run the risk of losing a good employee.

COMMISSION-BASED PAY FOR REGISTERED DIETITIANS

While your newly hired clinical Registered Dietitian/administrative employee is getting started, an hourly pay rate is appropriate. Once her client base has grown it is wise to switch this employee to commissions. You have given her the tools and financial support needed to excel, and now it is time to really have her earn what she is worth with commission-based pay. The earning potential can grow exponentially for the employee and your business can now reap the benefits.

Your Registered Dietitian who is earning commissions can also have the opportunity to earn additional income from her specialty programs, speaking engagements, product sales, administrative tasks, and special projects.

ADDITIONAL COMPENSATION FOR REGISTERED DIETITIANS

As the business owner, you can also set up additional employee perks to retain your best employees. Examples include:

- Reimbursement for travel, conferences, and continuing education
- Working with your financial adviser to set up a company retirement plan
- Provide health insurance
- Company cell phone, iPad, tablet, or computer that can also be for personal use
- Mileage reimbursement
- Pay for vacation and personal days

HOW TO MAKE IT WORK FOR THE BUSINESS AND FOR YOUR REGISTERED DIETITIANS

Each private practice is different, so think of win-win scenarios that might work for you. Can you pay the Registered Dietitian to help with growing your practice during non-client hours? Can the Registered Dietitian help to answer the phone, market your practice, give talks, create handouts, and call physicians' offices for referrals during her "downtime"? Remember that you want to keep this time to a minimum because it is not directly revenue generating for the practice. You might want to start your employee on an hourly basis to include time to do extra business tasks and see clients, and then convert to commissions once the Registered Dietitian starts to get a following and really learns how to grow and maintain a client base.

HAVE YOUR REGISTERED DIETITIANS BECOME INSURANCE PROVIDERS WHEN STARTING OUT

Earlier I said that having self-pay clients is best in terms of client success and financial stability for the Registered Dietitian. That is still true, but when you're starting out accepting insurance is very helpful, as it opens up a lot more business for your practice by attracting people who can be seen for nutrition counseling for little or no out-of-pocket expenses. Accepting insurance also increases your potential number of clients. That being said, there is no guarantee with insurance coverage regarding when or IF you will get paid for your services. You are taking a risk by only providing insurance-based appointments, which is why starting programs is important for your business' future.

When accepting insurance, your client base may be larger, but the pay is not stable nor is it consistent. Therefore, I would recommend offering insurance-based appointments, especially when starting out, while you develop more self-pay programs that will allow you to increase your income and create less frustration. Since insurance information and coverage is always changing, we have decided not to include the nitty-gritty details in this publication. For information on becoming an insurance provider, please reference our website at www.rbitzer.com or contact Dana@rbitzer.com directly, as she is our expert.

If you have decided to take insurance, there are many important things to consider. Here are some points I have learned along the way:

- At the initial visit you will need to make copies of the client's insurance card and driver's license in order to submit claims.
- It is important to gather information regarding ALL insurance plans (secondary and tertiary) even if the client is not using them for the visit.
- You will need to collect the full name, address, and date of birth of the primary beneficiary on the insurance plan. If a client's spouse or parent is the primary, you will need to get that information when scheduling the appointment.
- Medicare will only cover for diagnoses of diabetes or renal disease. All other diagnoses will be denied. If a client has Medicare and a secondary insurance you must, in most cases, submit the claim to Medicare even if you know it will not cover the diagnosis in order for the rejected claim to be sent by Medicare to the secondary insurance. There is also a limit to how many units (15 minute increments) the client can use for Medical Nutrition Therapy (MNT) each year.
- Medicaid will not cover MNT with a Registered Dietitian.
- Some insurance companies only cover a certain number of visits per calendar year. From experience, our team has learned how many visits the insurance will cover on average but it will differ with each client's insurance plan. When you notice trends such as three or six visits allowed each year, make it a policy to switch a client to self-pay once the visits have been denied.
- Diagnoses are important when determining insurance coverage. In our experience, diabetes, hypertension, and hypercholesterolemia are covered by most plans. Be advised that you can call for authorization with the insurance company before the visit; however, they do not guarantee any coverage (and in our experience they have verified MNT benefits and then denied the claim). If a client insists their insurance will cover the visit,

we ask them to check with their insurance company and verify that they are covered for MNT, with a Registered Dietitian in an outpatient setting, for their specific medical diagnosis. If they remain positive that insurance will guarantee coverage, we ask for a statement in writing from the insurance company to be faxed to our office.

- Weight loss, healthy eating, pre-diabetes, and vegetarianism are generally not covered diagnoses. These clients will have to be self-pay if they do not have another diagnosis.
- Copays: Medicare does not have a copayment. Other insurance companies will have copays and you should collect what is listed on their card under "S" for specialist. It is important to collect this at the time of service. Some plans do not have a copay listed. If there is a copay, it will be shown on the EOB (explanation of benefits) once you receive payment/denial.
- Participating providers are in a contractual agreement with the insurance company, which means they are obligated to bill and get a denial before telling the client the services are not covered. Make sure you have a policy clearly stated in your registration forms that if insurance does not pay for the visit the patient is responsible for payment of services.

Unfortunately, as you can imagine, this can be a time-consuming and frustrating experience for you and your clients. We have many tried and true tips that we have learned over the years to make this task more manageable. Although tedious, accepting insurance is an important client builder and it will expand your reach if you do it wisely. For more information on insurance such as diagnoses, copays, EOB's, and other reimbursement issues, please contact Dana (Dana@rbitzer.com) or visit our website at www.rbitzer.com.

Still not sure if you want to accept insurance? Here are some pros and cons to consider.

Pros of accepting insurance:

- It is an important client builder in order to fill your work schedule when starting up a practice or hiring new Registered Dietitians into the practice.
- Clients are happy using the insurance, as they pay for it throughout the year, and it allows them to afford consistent meetings with the Registered Dietitian.
- You can provide nutrition counseling to clients of all socioeconomic backgrounds.
- Insurance companies will list your name and contact information on their website when potential clients are searching for providers. This will receive a lot of traffic and act as a free marketing tool.
- Some insurance companies have wellness programs, which may pay you to speak at seminars or classes.

Cons of accepting insurance:

- Insurance coverage is inconsistent and preauthorization is often flawed.
- Clients are disgruntled when they believe insurance will cover and it does not.
- It may take multiple attempts to get payment for a specific claim. This can significantly affect your cash flow (more on this later).
- Insurance may ask you for a letter of medical necessity.
- Insurance may ask you for medical records.
- To accommodate the volume of work associated with accepting insurance it may be necessary to hire someone to do the billing to insurance.
- You or your employees will experience long wait times on the phone to address problem claims, often with little clarity.
- Payment for claims can take anywhere from a few weeks, to a few months, to a full year.
- Payment schedules for claims are lower than they have been in the past.
- If the insurance company pays you in error, they may take back your payment. Again, it is important to know the company policies, stay current, track your outcomes, and know what questions to ask. We can help you navigate this confusing and ever-changing insurance environment.

In Chapter 5 you will read more about how accepting insurance affects your revenue.

Inspiration from Rebecca: "When I first hired Kait as a full-time Registered Dietitian, the business took a huge hit. Even though she was generating income both counseling clients as a Registered Dietitian and by helping out with numerous administrative duties, she was definitely expensive. However, this investment in her was definitely a win-win scenario as she will explain. What made this decision easier was that I worked with her while she was a student and I was consistently impressed by her intelligence, ability to juggle many tasks, her passion, and her work ethic. I definitely wanted to make sure that she joined our team as a Registered Dietitian."

MY STORY

When I first found out about Rebecca Bitzer and Associates, a well-known, successful private practice that was only a short ride from my university, I knew I had to do whatever it took to get my foot in the door. I interviewed for a volunteer position while I was a sophomore dietetics major, promising to be organized and detail-oriented. I was hired, and at first, as expected, I was given tasks such as filing, scanning, conducting reminder calls, and various other secretarial duties. After excelling in the administrative side of things, I hungered for greater involvement with the nutrition side of the business. To prove that I was invested in the future of the business, I boldly started our famous RBA blog in 2009, created handouts, analyzed food logs for clients, and helped convey passion to potential clients at health fairs and community events.

Even throughout my entire 10-month, 40-hour week dietetic internship that took me away from RBA during the workweek, I devoted my time to RBA on Saturdays and week nights; I knew this place was too good to let go of. Despite all the other areas of dietetics I experienced, nothing called to me like the cutting-edge atmosphere at Rebecca Bitzer and Associates. Any visionary thoughts, dreams, or ideas I had were listened to and executed, and it was exciting to be around like-minded individuals. I conveyed this passion to Rebecca to secure a full-time position right out of my internship.

My only drawback was knowing how risky it could be to live on commission-only compensation right out of school with the financial responsibility of loans and bills. But Rebecca trusted my background as an intern who knew the ins and outs of scheduling appointments, the company's computer software, and other policies and procedures. She knew I could both see clients and work on administrative tasks while growing my client base on a full-time, entry-level salary.

Once I had a full client schedule and switched to commission, I DOUBLED my income and it has been everything I could dream of. This inspired me to work with Rebecca to pave the way for hiring Registered Dietitians with this win-win situation we created.

Together, we developed a mentorship track, working closely with the University of Maryland dietetics students to follow in my footsteps. We developed a thriving program of strong students, which led to strong Registered Dietitians. Since this program is so valuable to all of us, we would like to inspire you to do the same.

Inspiration from Rebecca: "I learned that when I first started interviewing applicants, I spent way too much time convincing the potential employee about all the benefits of working for RBA. I have now learned that this is not the most productive way to interview. The best way to evaluate future performance is to look at current performance. This being said, we have designed a brilliant way to hire our future Registered Dietitians that is based on their performance as volunteers. This functions as a one to two year interview for hiring as a full time Registered Dietitian."

HOW TO DEVELOP A MENTORSHIP TRACK FOR DIETETIC STUDENTS TO START VOLUNTEERING IN YOUR OFFICE

Students in a didactic dietetics programs are hungry for valuable experiences that enhance their resumes as they seek acceptance into the competitive world of dietetic internships. Hiring these students can be the perfect fit, bringing your practice new energy, new technology, and new passion. If you are not in proximity to a college or university with a dietetics program, think about hiring a student to work remotely for you instead. You can post your available positions on www.AllAccessInternships.com as well as send your information regarding the position to colleges and universities' dietetic student advisors or directors.

Rather than invest the money and time it takes to pay dietetic students from the start, set up a volunteer track as a trial period. It is hard to tell from one interview who will or will not be successful, so this trial period will allow you to retain great students and groom them into great Registered Dietitians.

The volunteer period is a top predictor for future job performance, so you can use this time to evaluate the student for future paid internships. Without seeing her performance as an administrative student, you will be less likely to take a risk and hire her as a full time Registered Dietitian. By getting to see a student in action, you will be able to see her strengths and drive in order to feel confident investing in her future.

Having such a mentorship track also helps you think long-term when hiring; therefore, try to interview freshmen and sophomores who will have a couple of years to grow with you. Consider a certain amount of hours volunteers are required to work. Over the years, RBA has found that six to eight hours a week allows volunteers the time to receive training, keep fresh with our ever-changing environment, and succeed in working on their assigned tasks. In order to make the transition from volunteer to employee, RBA uses a quiz to evaluate if they are indeed ready to move on to becoming a paid student. For more information about this mentorship track please visit our website at www.rbitzer.com.

When you are selective and slow to hire, your practice will attract excellent staff and Registered Dietitians. RBA is extremely proud to say that our last eleven students have been chosen for an accredited dietetic internship, giving us a 100% match rate of any interns who have applied. This is truly an impressive feat with the national average of a 50% match rate. (http://www.allaccessinternships.com/GettingMatched.AGuideforDieteticsStudents.pdf).

As of this writing, RBA currently has three Registered Dietitians who started as students and we have a goal to hire two more Registered Dietitians next year. Rebecca, Dana, and I believe that dietetics is a profession based on paying it forward. Our field is dominated by women and we tend to be excellent helpers, planners, and networkers. Applying this to employees has allowed RBA to have an administrative staff of ten; stay current with nutrition knowledge, technology, and social media; and broaden our reach.

ADMINISTRATIVE VOLUNTEERS/ INTERNS IN ACTION

The great thing is that once your students or newly hired Registered Dietitians have been trained administratively, they can come on to your team wearing different hats. Here are some tasks they can help with administratively while getting paid hourly and increasing their client base:

- Business-Related Tasks
    - Hire and train employees, Registered Dietitians, and dietetic students.
    - Manage intern schedules and daily tasks.
    - Assist with the business side of things: tracking appointments and business statistics, running payroll reports, checking balances, and making bank deposits.
    - Coordinate monthly Registered Dietitian meetings.
    - Update policies and procedures.
    - Oversee all administrative tasks.
    - Investigate new revenue streams.
    - Plan open houses and team building events.
    - Manage insurance and billing procedures.

- Client-Related Tasks
  - Schedule appointments.
  - Become an insurance provider to allow for greater client base (more on this later).
  - Create and update your nutrition handouts.
  - Personally contact clients each week to follow up on their appointments.
  - Run weekly support groups or classes.
  - Monitor e-mail lists for relevant nutrition research and trends pertaining to your practice.
  - Conduct grocery store tours.
- Marketing-Tasks
  - Work community health fairs for greater exposure for your practice.
  - Create brochures and bulletin boards.
  - Run reports of physicians, therapists, trainers, and other referral sources in your area.
  - Visit physicians' offices and gyms to introduce your practice and your Registered Dietitians.
- Social Media Tasks
  - Create a blogging and social media schedule to help with marketing.
  - Schedule tweets and Facebook posts.
  - Write monthly newsletters.

Inspiration from Dana: "Starting as an administrative student intern at RBA allowed me to be proficient in all aspects of client care, from scheduling the appointment to working as a Registered Dietitian. This experience allowed me to be a better supervisor, as I have performed all tasks that I now delegate to our student team. I am able to help streamline these tasks as well as celebrate their triumphs and understand their challenges."

The possibilities are endless for these key employees who can strengthen the health of your overall business and ultimately generate client-based revenue. As the owner, you need to be clear in assigning tasks to your Registered Dietitians. Remember, initially your Registered Dietitians will do more than consult with clients. They will need to perform every task in the office to get up-to-speed and succeed in private practice.

Developing a strong mentorship track that leads to hiring successful Registered Dietitians also contributes to the longevity of your practice. Your business could be self-sustainable and running with the help of your employees without you having to be involved in the day-to-day tasks. No one person is irreplaceable since they have been trained in every system and task, which allows you as the business owner to take time off and work on big picture goals, quality assurance, and mentoring. It is important for you to have uninterrupted time to develop programs, marketing campaigns, and employee training and retention.

Inspiration from Dana: "Invest in your Registered Dietitians' futures because you are also investing in your business and your retirement. This is also a nice perk for your top Registered Dietitians, as an investment opportunity later on in their career. For example, I am more likely to stay with RBA long-term because RBA invests in my continuing education, my retirement, offers the potential to buy into the business, and has my best interests at heart. This position offers so much more than just an hourly or commission-based wage, which prompts our Registered Dietitians to stay."

VOLUNTEER BENEFITS

Your office can provide nutrition and business opportunities for your volunteers that will enrich their education with real life experience in the field and benefit their career as a Registered Dietitian. Examples include:

- Learning the ins and outs of the business of dietetics
- Receiving bonuses for scheduling visits or completing projects
- Awarding "Student of the Month" and featuring this employee on your blog and website
- Blogging and developing a social media portfolio
- Receiving LinkedIn recommendations and recommendations for dietetic internships

- Getting paired up with a Registered Dietitian who can mentor and share nutrition knowledge with them
- Attending administrative and clinical meetings monthly to learn from the Registered Dietitians
- Learning from case studies and sitting in for counseling sessions, with permission from the client. This enables them to evaluate if being a Registered Dietitian in private practice is a good career fit.
- Potential to move up the ranks to become a paid student and ultimately employed as an RBA Registered Dietitian

QUOTES AND INSPIRATION FROM OUR STUDENT INTERNS AND VOLUNTEERS

"I've learned more from my mentors at RBA than I have at any other place. The collegiate environment and everywhere else I have worked does not allow a mentor/mentee relationship to develop. I think that I'm ten times more prepared than other students for the application process from this mentor/mentee relationship, especially since Kait and Dana were there to help me. Working with all my mentors at RBA made me a better future Registered Dietitian and inspires me every day to work as hard as possible toward my goals." – Alex

"You could tell the Registered Dietitians truly cared about their patients and that caring nature trickled down to the students as well. It's a win-win for everyone! Student experience can be very hard to come by. The students will be forever grateful AND you have employees who are actually interested in what you are doing and actually want to work on projects for you!" – Chelsea

"I think what I like most is that all the Registered Dietitians at RBA are so enthusiastic and truly love their jobs. This had me so excited to become a Registered Dietitian. I know that I am a "hands-on" learner and I learn so much more at RBA than I ever would have just sitting in a classroom. I believe that the student interns at RBA will truly become leaders among other entry level Registered Dietitians because of the mentoring from the Registered Dietitians at RBA." – Shelby

"I can honestly say that each and every RBA Registered Dietitian wanted to make the office a positive learning experience for all of the student interns. They were all willing and happy to answer any and all questions that I had. I also got to sit in on a couple of consultations, which really helped me get an inside peak of what working at a private practice would be like." – Haley

"I learned so much about the behind-the-scenes work of the Registered Dietitian: reimbursement, social media, coordination of care, and consulting. Rebecca taught me about the benefits of networking and showed me what it takes to be a successful entrepreneur—instead of fearing change, revel in it. Students are not only motivated volunteers and employees, but they are also your future colleagues and potential change makers. You can have a hand in molding the future of dietetics through your work with students." – Debi

TRAINING ALONG THE MENTORSHIP TRACK

Now that you have some wonderful employees and volunteers, it is important to keep up with ongoing training and retention. Effective training will foster successful future Registered Dietitians for your business.

One of the most challenging parts of running a busy group practice in the ever-changing economy, technology, human resources, and insurance climate is making sure that everyone is on the same page with the "how to's" of every single activity.

Inspiration from Rebecca: "My business coach helped me realize the importance of sitting down and writing out all policies and procedures in one large document for running the business. The three main reasons for doing so are: 1) To spend less time discussing problems and solutions over and over again that would come up repeatedly, but not often enough to remember how it was solved it the previous time. 2) To help you as the business owner step away from the practice for more balance in life (self-care). 3) To ultimately set up your business to sell or bring on a partner to leave a legacy and/or to fund your retirement."

Putting together a policy and procedure manual has been priceless. We have an ever-growing copy of this manual on our computers and in a printed form (for times when the internet is down or we lose power). This book took months to write but has helped us tremendously.

Now is the time to start writing down your own policy and procedure manual. You will be amazed by all the details of running your business. Since this is such a big task, you might want to start small and document everything new that you put into place in your practice. This will help you in terms of running your day-to-day practice, training new employees, and having a formal "corporate memory" of what was done in the past.

Also, maintaining this manual is a great job to delegate to a newer employee, as it is essential that the new employee keeps up with all the ins and outs of running the business. Like most things, writing everything down is a big chore, but it is very much worth the effort in the long run. We call it a *playbook*, instead of a policy and procedure manual, because playbook at least seems more fun.

Having a playbook is a great way for you to ensure that everyone is trained consistently and up-to-date on new changes. It also enables you to have a unified resource with current information, updated weekly. Once you have systems in place, you will be able to rest assured that you can go on vacation without staying connected to the business 24/7 or worry whether things are running smoothly. Once we had this in place, our staff could more easily answer questions and stay consistent without asking Rebecca, Dana, or me the more easily-answered questions.

In terms of the playbook, here are ideas of what you may want to include in yours:

- Organizational chart showing hierarchy of employees
- Job descriptions of each employee
- "Cheat Sheets" that can be placed near each phone with information regarding insurance, Registered Dietitian information, scheduling appointments, and other Electronic Health Record procedures
- Student and administrative responsibilities: reminder calls, ordering supplies, and contacting new and inactive clients
- Marketing and business opportunities: social media goals, contact lists, and referral sources
- Contact information: employee phone lists, provider ID numbers, passwords, and account numbers
- Checklists to make sure systems are followed

Since having a playbook is such an important quality assurance and training tool, you may want to study the outline of our playbook below to inspire you to create your own. Your playbook will always be evolving and should be updated to reflect additions or changes to protocols. Many small businesses do not have a playbook, but it is worth the time and effort, so the sooner you start the sooner you will be well on your way to streamlining your business.

Here is the table of contents from our playbook:

REBECCA BITZER & ASSOCIATES PLAYBOOK TABLE OF CONTENTS

FOR MORE INFORMATION:
WWW.RBITZER.COM

In addition to the playbook, it is equally important to have an employee manual. Your employee manual can be part of your playbook or a separate document. Your employee manual (or handbook) would primarily cover policies and procedures about your employer/employee relationship. As the owner, you are responsible for creating an employee manual and appropriate employee forms, including:

- Employee Policies
- Employee Job Description
- Employee Benefits Agreement
- Company Policies
- Employee Protocols
- Employee Review (Evaluation) Forms
- Employee Separations

For more information visit our website at www.rbitzer.com.

You will want to have your employee manual and any forms approved by your attorney, and the manual should be signed by your employees yearly.

SAMPLE OF REBEL DIETITIANS IN ACTION

Now that you have yourself and your employees more organized, you can spend time on other activities. Not everything REBEL Dietitians do is one-on-one counseling. There's a lot of business savvy and outreach involved.

So what exactly does a REBEL Dietitian do all day? The following pie chart can give you some insight on how you may structure your daily/weekly/monthly activity.

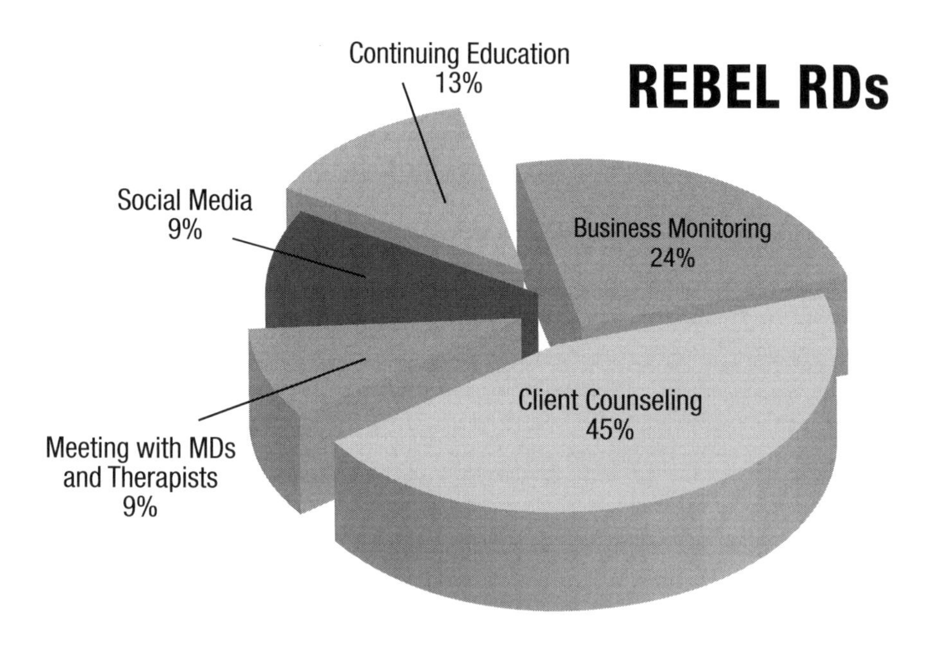

For more information visit our website at www.rbitzer.com.

COMMUNICATION BETWEEN REGISTERED DIETITIANS AND ADMINISTRATIVE STUDENTS VOLUNTEERS/INTERNS

Have constant communication with your employees in an organized fashion to prevent problems. Here are some things to incorporate into your communication strategy:

- Send out a weekly staff newsletter with policy changes, updates, and announcements and then have someone add to the playbook weekly.
- Develop a template for a daily task sheet that students can fill out to indicate what they have completed once their shift is over (electronic or handwritten) to be monitored by their supervisor.
- Meet with your business team weekly/monthly/quarterly to discuss clients' account issues, relevant projects, budgeting, and planning of the entire business.
- Have weekly/monthly Registered Dietitian meetings to celebrate successes and share struggles. We blend our Registered Dietitian meetings with a discussion of the logistics of running our practice, updates in policies, new programs, electronic medical records, and nutrition education by sharing case studies and research articles. We currently meet virtually using Google Chat once per month and each Registered Dietitian takes a turn presenting a case study as a form of peer supervision.

- Block off lunch time to collaborate with dietetic interns and Registered Dietitians to discuss personal self-care and trending nutrition topics. These experiences can lead to fun and helpful blog posts.
- Conduct team building events such as trips or hands-on cooking opportunities to foster collaboration and build relationships.
- Develop a gratitude jar in your office that everyone can contribute to in order to show thanks for others in your office.
- Working as a team, you can consistently share TED Talks, articles, electronic mailing list posts, and audiobooks to take advantage of "down time" both for personal and professional inspiration. The key is always staying focused on your vision and embracing takeaways.

REVENUE STREAMS

Now that you have hired the *right* people and have excellent protocols lined up, you are set to have a strong revenue stream through individual counseling. However, you do not want to rely solely on one-on-one counseling as your only source of income, because it increases your risk. For instance, if you build your practice accepting Blue Cross Blue Shield insurance and they suddenly stop reimbursing for nutrition counseling, you are in trouble.

So what else can you do to bring in revenue? Aside from hiring more Registered Dietitians, here are some other avenues to explore:

- Speaking Engagements: Create a speaker request form for your website that allows interested parties to fill out their time and location, expected attendance, topic idea, and budget requirements. By having this filled out ahead of time you will be prepared with which Registered Dietitian can do the job and what your compensation will be. While you may want to volunteer for various organizations, you cannot provide every free talk requested. Think about location and clientele you will be reaching to provide you with a source of referrals who are interested in your services. You may also choose to barter for payment. For instance, you may give a free talk in a school if

Dana Magee presenting at the University of Maryland about how to REBEL against dieting.

they are able to use their audiovisual equipment to professionally record some clips of your talk that you can upload to your website. Or they may be able to feature you on their website to broaden your reach.

- Sublet office space to other health professionals.
- Testing for clients: You can charge for these services and they help provide credibility to your practice while giving patients scientific information and measurable results. Some tests include:
  - Metabolic testing to determine resting energy expenditure
  - Body fat testing
  - Food sensitivity testing
  - Cardiovascular risk testing (Boston Heart Diagnostics)
- Distribute vitamins and other nutrition supplements (Make sure you only recommend products you believe in.)
- Conduct menu analysis for various organizations and restaurants.
- Resources produced by the Registered Dietitians.
- Selling products you recommend on your website or in your office: Cookbooks, pedometers, water bottles, kitchen equipment, and professional workbooks or books you love. Be aware of sales tax laws in your state.
- Business coaching. Once you find something that works for you, empower other Registered Dietitians by providing business coaching opportunities. Our REBEL team has helped many Registered Dietitians face their fears and advance their careers.

EXPANDING TO ANOTHER OFFICE

Another way you can help a greater number of clients and grow your practice is to diversify locations. You may have outgrown your space or perhaps you just want to expand. Of course, if you are hiring new employees who now have a greater client base, you'll definitely want to consider expanding locations.

A new location brings access to a different clientele who may not be able (or willing) to travel to your other location. Additionally, it is wise to have offices in different socioeconomic areas in order to reach a wider demographic. As noted, seeing clients with health insurance can help build your practice and can lead to more up-selling. Often, you can transition this client to a self-pay program once insurance benefits expire.

As you think about expanding, here are some different options to consider.

Owning your own office suite

Owning your own office or suite can increase your professionalism and credibility. It will also allow you the freedom to use your space in multiple ways, whether that is hiring Registered Dietitians to fill all of the rooms, using the space for meetings and events, or renting out empty rooms to other professionals when they are available. This can act as another source of income if you are investing in your property versus paying rent. If you own the property, when it's paid off it can be a nice nest egg or future income stream if you sell or rent at a later date.

Here is a peek into one of our warm and inviting offices. While there is a computer in the room, clients will sit on the couch and our Registered Dietitians sit directly across from them in session to help open communication.

Being part of a shared suite

You may choose to share an office suite with a collection of health professionals. This option facilitates cross referring with other professionals in the building. Sharing a suite may also allow you to share the associated fees including rent, internet, support staff, office equipment, and supplies.
Keep in mind that all decisions must be discussed with all the professionals in the suite and there may be resistance to some of your ideas, such as hosting a food sensitivity blood draw in the office.

Being in a physician's office

Physicians may approach you to have hours weekly or monthly in their office to serve their clients. This may be a great way to start out and build relationships with physicians. Be aware that this may seem like an endless referral source due to a large client pool, but if many of your referrals come from a variety of physicians it may be limiting. If you do share an office, make sure to have your own separate identity and branding. It is also difficult to have the proper setting as a guest in another office.

Additional things to think about when setting up in a physician's office:

- Will you have access to the printer or fax machine?
- What will the physical set up be?
- Will you be set up in a patient exam room instead of a counseling room?

- Will you have to cart your materials around with you from office to office?
- Will you have direct contact with the providers and be invited to their provider meetings so they know you are there providing services?
- What is the pay arrangement?

HOW TO KEEP YOUR VARIOUS OFFICES ALIGNED

When you have more than one office, keeping all your staff aligned and on the same page can be a challenge. Here are some ways to keep communication strong between offices so you truly are a unified company and not separate entities.

- Use password protected web pages and Google Drive to share handouts and important forms from any location with your staff.
- Electronic health records allow all charts to be accessed from any location as well as billing information, payments, and scheduling follow up appointments. Be sure to stay Health Insurance Portability and Accountability Act (HIPAA) compliant.
- Train administrative staff to know all locations and set ups, even if they are not physically in that office.

REBEL SUCCESS STRATEGIES

ASSIGNMENTS:

- [ ] Set up meetings with an attorney, accountant, and financial advisor to get all your legal and finance-related tasks organized.
- [ ] Complete a time study on yourself. From the results, do you need to hire an administrative student, Registered Dietitian, or a Registered Dietitian that can do both counseling and administrative work? What tasks would you like the Registered Dietitian to work on administratively while growing her client base? Write a job description based on these results.

____

____

____

____

____

☐ Look into a university or dietetics program in your area with whom you can work with to start a mentorship track.

____

____

____

____

☐ Start a playbook and employee manual with everything you have worked on thus far. Include your job descriptions, employee forms, and most importantly, your mission.

____

____

____

____

____

☐ Are you ready to expand to another location? Do you have more Registered Dietitians than can fit in your available space? Research the area you are looking to expand to and determine the demographics to see if they are a fit for your specialty and pricing.

____

____

____

____

____

"You can do anything, but not everything all at once."

– David Allen

REBEL RD

CHAPTER FOUR

E – Empower Your Clients to Be Successful and Happy

Create Client Protocols for Consistent Customer Service

If you're like most Registered Dietitians, you chose this field because of your passion for helping others. Every single call and client is extremely important. Therefore, you will want to make sure that every client has the best experience possible. Doing that requires that you have systems in place for consistency. This quality assurance measure ensures that your clients receive the same high quality experience from their first phone call to their first appointment and beyond. Having client policies and procedures enables others to perceive you in the best light possible, which will generate successful clients, great reviews, and positive word of mouth … leading to more sales!

A nutrition appointment can be very scary for certain individuals; there are few things as personal to most people as food is. Whether it is stemming from tradition, culture, shame or guilt about overeating, emotional eating, disordered eating, or digestive issues, you always want to treat your clients with respect and compassion. After all, clients are the heart of your practice, and their first impression of you is a lasting one. This starts the minute they find you.

SETTING UP CLIENT APPOINTMENTS FROM START TO FINISH

Potential clients should be able to learn about you via your website. Visiting a website for initial information is much easier than (and not as scary as) calling for information. Therefore, make sure you have a link to a request form on your site where your clients can enter their information and request an appointment. This link should allow clients to directly contact you by email.

By having this option on your website, it gives your clients the opportunity to learn more about you before even making that initial contact. On this form, potential clients will fill out the necessary information such as their name, birth date, address, reason for their appointment or inquiry, and insurance information (which you'll need to make their appointment in your scheduling system). Another advantage to this form is that you'll have the details about their situation in front of you before you call them and can present them the best options. This will help your team feel more prepared in scheduling the appointment, and the phone call will go more smoothly.

Set this form up so the site sends prospects a "thank you" message immediately upon sending their information or question to you (this is called an autoresponder). This message should also let potential clients know that their inquiry has been received and someone from your office will call them back shortly.

However, not all initial contacts will start with a website inquiry. Many people will call your office with initial questions. If you personally are not answering the phone when the client calls, your administrative staff needs to warmly and knowledgeably communicate your company's mission and expertise. Create a phone script that can help your staff feel at ease and confidently answer clients' questions. Make sure to include screening questions based on clients' needs, commonly asked questions, or vital information for new clients, such as:

- The reason they are seeking nutrition services
- What to bring to their first appointment
- Insurance and payment options
- Length and number of visits
- What the first meeting will entail

Here are some tips for your staff:

- If the client doesn't immediately tell you, ask what they are coming in for so you can get an idea of which Registered Dietitian and program is the best match for the client. Do NOT ask about insurance until you have talked to the client a little more. *You don't want to turn them away right at the beginning if insurance does not cover the appointment.*
- Ask them how they heard about you (physician, friend, website, blog, etc.).
- Ask questions to build rapport. What do they feel their biggest challenge is in regard to their diet or eating habits right now? What have they tried in the past? What are their nutrition goals?

- Inform the client of the appropriate Registered Dietitian for their needs. Tell her which days the Registered Dietitian is in and ask which times are best. Discuss any applicable package or specialty program.
- When someone calls requesting a specific Registered Dietitian or seems to be a good candidate for one of the specialty programs, take some time to explain the program components with emphasis on the additional add-ons that would not be included in a standard session.
- With the client on the phone, fill out a new client information form, which prompts your staff to acquire all the necessary demographic information and anything unique the Registered Dietitian may need to know. You can find a copy of our form on our website at www.rbitzer.com.

Your administrative team is responsible for matching each client with the Registered Dietitian for their needs based on diagnosis, scheduling, office location, and payment/insurance method. By matching these clients with the best Registered Dietitian for them at the start, you can ensure happier and more successful clients.

Inspiration from Rebecca: "As the business owner, I find that it is sometimes difficult to step away from the business and learn to delegate, although this is essential if you want to bring your best to the business for the long haul. Additionally, it is essential to develop strong systems of doing things so you can be assured that your practice will run smoothly and efficiently. For example, it's very unprofessional if someone calls the office and gets conflicting answers to their questions. Having systems in place will also enable you to better groom the next generation to one day take over the business and bring it to an even higher level than you ever dreamt possible."

ASSURING YOUR CLIENTS MAKE IT TO THE FIRST APPOINTMENT

Once the appointment is scheduled, send clients a confirmation email with a warm welcome message, the date and time of the appointment, a list of what to bring to the appointment, information on how to cancel or reschedule, and directions to your office. This can be saved as a template on your computer. Also attach the necessary new client registration forms for them to fill out prior to their appointment.

Each day, have an experienced member of your administrative team check all new appointments to double check for any errors. The goal is to make sure your clients are matched with the appropriate Registered Dietitian, verify payment and insurance information, and confirm the location and time. This ensures there are no "surprises" when clients arrive. Train your staff to initial each form so you know who to talk to when there may be a question.

To limit the amount of no-shows, remind clients via phone or email two days before their appointment. Also, consider scheduling new client appointments during less popular times and save high priority times (early morning and evening) for your reliable, returning clients.

THE IMPORTANCE OF THE NEW CLIENT REGISTRATION FORM

Ideally, clients will have already filled out your registration form, which the staff can upload to each client's electronic chart. You can email the form to clients prior to their appointment, have it available as a download on your website, or snail mail it to them. If the clients have not filled out the form prior to arriving, have them fill it out while in the waiting room before seeing the Registered Dietitian. It is important for these forms to be filled out prior to working with new clients so you are both as prepared as possible for the appointment.

The registration form should have a section with medical history, medications, symptoms, important questions about their nutrition and health struggles, and what results they want. By bringing these points to their attention, clients can better commit to working with you. Additionally, as the Registered Dietitian, you can be prepared to provide the best care possible.

Be sure your policies are clearly and completely written out on the form for clients to sign. Your Registered Dietitians must confirm that these policies have been signed. If a client chooses not to sign the policies, emphasize that this is your policy and they need to be completed in order to be seen. The client must also fill in the details of their insurance information.

Inspiration from Rebecca: "Paying attention to the nitty-gritty details in advance and overseeing that everything is done consistently will save you much time in the long run."

It is helpful to have different registration forms based upon your programs or specialties. By individualizing your questions to fit the clients' specific needs, you will be able to help clients identify the need for nutrition counseling, and you will be able to discuss how you can help find solutions for the clients' problems. Examples of our individualized registration forms include: Anorexia Nervosa (AN), Bulimia Nervosa (BN), Binge Eating Disorder (BED), Avoidant / Restrictive Food Intake Disorder (ARFID), Digestive and, Polycystic Ovarian Syndrome (PCOS).

For a sample of registration form visit our website at www.rbitzer.com.

DURING THE FIRST APPOINTMENT

Meet your clients where they are on their journey and focus on what they want to get out of your time together. At this point, connecting and building rapport with the client is the priority. You want them to trust you and tell you what is really going on so that you can best help them.

Make sure you have adequate time to spend with clients and really listen to what they are telling you. This first session is essential for setting the tone for a long-term relationship. Stress to your clients that this is not a quick fix, and you will be working together to help them meet their goals.

Inspiration from Rebecca: "Just as you develop your technical skills and stay up-to-date on the latest nutrition research, you also need to develop your counseling and people skills. Remember that clients want more than just facts from you; they are also seeking compassion, connection, and care. Therefore, seek out training in such things as communication and people skills. This will help ensure that you develop long-term clients rather than one-time appointments."

Inspiration from Dana: "A common mistake I used to make is giving too much information in my first session. My young age prompted me to overcompensate and provide too many nutrition facts to prove my expertise. I now take the time to really listen to clients and only give them bite-sized pieces of information."

Here are some key points to keep in mind during this and future appointments:

- During sessions, remember to be attentive, kind, and non-judgmental. Don't be afraid of silence, and let your client be comfortable with feeling emotions.
- Make sure to focus on helping your clients get results. Results turn into conversations with friends and family and are a great way to get referrals. Keep in mind that results

are also things outside of weight loss or management. Examples include forming a better relationship with food, learning to cook family meals, decreasing reliance on medication, lowering cholesterol, incorporating self-care, increasing energy, and/or just *feeling* better.

- Ending your session is just as important. Work with your clients to set clear, achievable goals.
- Emphasize the importance of a follow-up appointment every one to two weeks at first while embarking upon a lifestyle change. As the Registered Dietitian, take responsibility in scheduling the follow up with the clients rather than your staff. Once they have become long-term clients, remind them that follow-ups every one to three months are also important as changes in season, holidays, family, or job stress can easily change your clients' routines.

INTRODUCING YOUR CLIENTS TO YOUR PROGRAM

In chapter two, you outlined and created a program for your ideal client based on your area of expertise. If the person sitting in front of you is a match for your program, now is the time to discuss how it can help them get the results they are seeking. Your staff may have introduced the program over the phone; it is your turn to convey your passion for your program. While this is technically a sales opportunity, don't think of it as selling. You're simply offering your clients the services they need to improve their lives and reach their goals.

As you talk with your clients about your program, keep these points in mind:

- Restate the client's "pain." Find out how their eating is affecting their life in terms of the time spent thinking about food, weight, health, and body image. Also find out how this is affecting their money, time, energy, and relationships, or preventing them from living a full, meaningful life.
- After emphasizing the client's challenges, explain how you can help. Select the specific challenges that working with you can address and how that will benefit them financially, emotionally, and personally.
- If a client is interested but says s/he cannot afford the program, remove the money block. Ask, "If we did not have to discuss money, would there be anything holding you back from signing up today?" Typically, money is not the real reason why people don't sign up. It's something else but they're using "no money" as the excuse. Asking this question helps to air out what the real objection, fear, or hesitation is. For more tips on how to navigate this common scenario, please contact us.

- Walk clients through all the support and add-ons included in your program. Always do this process during a paid, in-person screening so you set the professional tone.
- Remember, it is your responsibility to help clients understand the value of your services.

FOLLOWING UP WITH YOUR CLIENTS

Just because clients leave your office doesn't mean you're done with them until the next visit. Quite the contrary! You and your staff still have much to do.

First, with your clients' written permission, connect with their other health professionals, including physicians, therapists, and psychiatrists, and keep them posted on your shared clients' progress. Not only is this a great way to obtain other referrals, but it also helps keep clients accountable to their nutrition appointments.

A few days after the appointment, reach out to your new clients for feedback. For example, after the first appointment, email each client something similar to the following:

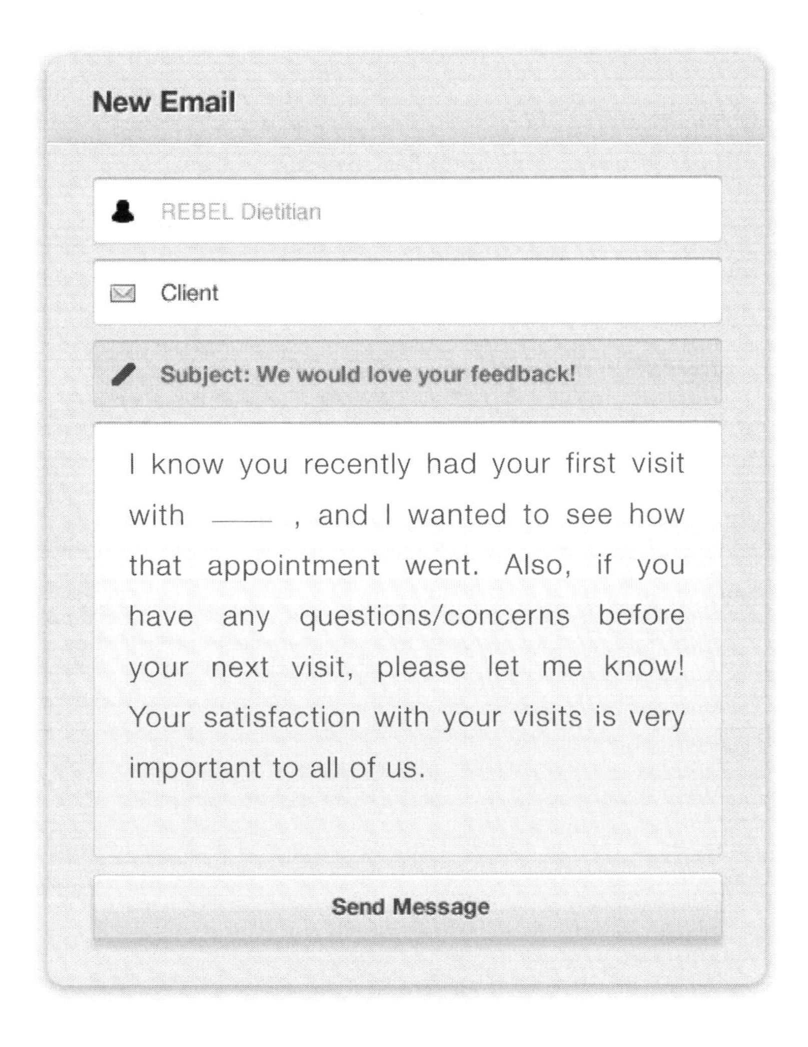

This allows you to gather testimonials for positive feedback or catch any unhappy clients right away to ensure that you can keep them coming back for their appointments.

For returning clients, email them a nutrition preparation form as discussed previously in chapter two. For a sample of one, please see our website at www.rbitzer.com.

Offering phone and email support for a small fee or included as part of a program also allows your clients to feel connected to you as their personal nutritionist and is great for busy clients who may not be able to come in each week. It's like having a personal nutritionist 24/7. However, make sure to set appropriate boundaries on email support. If the email contains a lot of questions or a new development comes up, this is a great opportunity to emphasize the importance of meeting more frequently.

Finally, make sure to touch base with clients who missed their appointment or have not scheduled a follow up. For inactive clients, you will want to create an email template to reach those who have not been in your office for six months to see if they would like to make another appointment. Perhaps they were not initially ready to make a change or have been falling off track since their last meeting. Let them know about new classes/programs/groups to show them that you continue to improve your offerings.

For examples of our phone script, email templates, and nutrition preparation form, visit our website at www.rbitzer.com.

CLIENT PRIVACY AND PROTECTION

The Health Insurance Portability and Accountability Act (HIPAA) is federally mandated regulation designed to protect personal information and data collected and stored in medical records. HIPAA was established as a national standard to be used in all physicians' offices, hospitals, and other businesses where personal medical information is stored. In addition to protecting personal medical information, HIPAA also gives patients the right to view their medical records and request changes if the data is incorrect. Be diligent with enforcing HIPAA compliance in your office.

Why?

- To protect your clients: You work in a very personal field and protecting your clients' personal information, including their identity, their medical information, their food information, and your confidential intervention with them, is essential.
- To protect yourself: HIPAA laws are getting more and more stringent. It is important to follow what's happening in order to keep from incurring a fine or losing clients if information is mishandled.

Here are some important points regarding HIPAA for your office:

- We strongly recommend that you have your employees pass a HIPAA training and quiz for the protection of your clients.
- Your employees must sign a HIPAA agreement.
- Clients must sign your HIPAA policy.
- Clients must sign a release form allowing you to communicate with physicians and other members on the treatment team.
- Always use safe methods of information transmittance: fax, snail mail, electronic health records (EHR), or encrypted email.
- Shred any document with client information. You can use a shredding service or a small office shredder.
- For your email and electronic health records, be sure to change your passwords each month.
- Establish disciplinary protocol if any employee violates HIPAA.

ELECTRONIC HEALTH RECORDS (EHR)

Convert to electronic health records sooner rather than later. EHR can provide huge benefits to help streamline your practice, as scheduling, billing, and charting are all located in one place, essentially taking three different systems and replacing them with one, allowing you more time to enjoy your REBELution.

Scheduling

- You can look at your schedule ahead of time to see why clients are coming in so you can best prepare for your session.
- You can set up recurring appointments for weekly clients and business meetings.
- You will have availability of all providers' locations and hours in one schedule.

Charting

- You can customize your clients' notes with individualized templates specific to your Registered Dietitian's ideal charting requirements. For instance, you can set up user-friendly fields to collect names and contact information of treatment team professionals, symptoms of eating disorders, significant medical history, medications, adherence to food plans, milestones accomplished, etc. All of this information can also be designed to be easily tracked for progress. For convenience, you are also able to add necessary information from the previous appointment. For an example of our charting templates, please visit our website at www.rbitzer.com.

- You can track and graph vitals such as height and weight, and you can upload labs to your clients' charts to make you a more results-oriented Registered Dietitian.
- You can easily add progress or discharge notes from other health professionals.
- You can review clients' notes safely from all of your locations.
- To further your clients' protection, you can use their assigned client identification number from your EHR system instead of referring to clients by name or initials when problem solving accounts receivable with the billing manager.
- You can set alerts on your client's charts to pop up when the chart has been opened to remind you of outstanding balances, health history, goals, or to personalize your sessions with a fun fact you want to remember about the client.
- You can securely contact your clients via email through a HIPAA safe patient portal within your EHR system.
- You can print professional progress notes to share with referring physicians and other professionals on clients' treatment teams with a signed release.
- You can save time and money by not having to file charts, as well as save money on paper and folders.
- You can increase storage space in your office with less charts and paper to be stored, which will help you declutter.

Billing

- You can keep all insurance information on file and track the status of reimbursement.
- You can directly accept credit card payments with a magnetic credit card reader linked to your EHR.
- You can directly enter checks and cash into the system and apply it to clients' accounts.
- You can check balances before your clients' appointments.
- You can view your clients' payments and visit history.

- You can create superbills and submit claims through the EHR, which is further motivation to do your billing in-house.
- You can easily run reports for all the statistics you value. This includes appointment reports, patient visit reports, claims and billing reports, and accounting reports. You can run these reports daily, weekly, monthly, or yearly. You may choose to run them categorized by Registered Dietitian or by office location as well (more on this later).

LEARNING CURVES WITH EHR

Of course, there is a lot of work that goes into making this major switch. As a private practice you may not be required by deadline to convert; however, it is best to do this sooner rather than later and take advantage of this great advance in technology. You may find your newly-employed Registered Dietitian to be helpful in making this switch as she has the time to devote to the conversion and may have experienced transitioning to or using EHR during her internship in the hospital setting.

Realize that until your EHR is fully functional you may be juggling paper and learning the entirely new computerized system. It is best to make the conversion as quickly as possible so nothing falls through the cracks during the transition. Remember your administrative staff and Registered Dietitians will need training on all of the new policies and functions that come with this technology. To make it easier, I recommend starting with the billing and scheduling portion of the system you choose, which is often free to use. Then transition to the online charting as part of the next phase. This will allow you to get comfortable with your system, enter all your patient data, and start using the software in stages without overwhelming yourself and your staff.

Another barrier to consider is that typing up notes in session at a desk behind a computer can be impersonal. You do not want to handwrite your notes and double the work by later typing them into your electronic notes. To conquer this, RBA has purchased tablets that can be used in session to write the notes without our backs to our clients. With the tablet we can face the clients, and the smaller screen does not interfere with us creating rapport and building connection while counseling clients.

However, when the network, EHR, or internet is down you will be essentially flying blind. Therefore, consider a data plan for your tablet or back up internet provider to prevent this issue.

Finally, there is a monthly fee for each Registered Dietitian using EHR. The rate is the same regardless of how many clients your Registered Dietitian is seeing. To help with the expenses, you might start with your Registered Dietitians with the highest volume of clients to help with efficiency. Having protocols in place for client care, privacy, and documentation will allow your office to run smoothly so you can truly focus on the clients' needs in session and empower them to be successful. Your clients will know what to expect and can trust you to provide the best care possible.

REBEL SUCCESS STRATEGIES

ASSIGNMENTS

- [ ] Make a phone script for your administrative staff. (Visit our website at www.rbitzer.com for an example.)

____

____

____

____

____

- [ ] Develop three effective email templates for new, current, and inactive clients to achieve greater retention. Set these up using saved templates in your email platform.

____

____

____

____

____

____

____

____

____

- [ ] Sign up for a free training with an EHR system to see if it will work for your practice. We use Office Ally.

"You are not here merely to make a living. You are here in order to enable the world to live more amply, with greater vision, with a finer spirit of hope and achievement. You are here to enrich the world, and you impoverish yourself if you forget the errand."

– Woodrow Wilson

REBEL RD

CHAPTER FIVE

L – Learn Ways to Keep Your Practice Financially Successful

Tracking and Budgeting: Nutrition Counseling Business 101

Running a private practice does not require you to have a business degree; however, knowing the basics of finance and accounting are a must. As I discussed earlier, it is important to have people helping you, but you need to be educated enough to know what's going on in your business and to be able ask the right questions. Tracking your business' progress is key to your success. Additionally, it's always important to have your finger on the pulse of your business to evaluate trends. Tracking enables you to do this. Most small businesses have a profit of three to five percent, so it is important to set goals to meet or beat this percentage.

Inspiration from Rebecca: "You may be under the impression that your business is doing well because you are booked solid, but be aware that just because your office is busy it does not guarantee you are making a profit. That's why it is essential to track all aspects of your business."

TRACKING YOUR BUSINESS

Tracking may not sound very rebellious or fun, but you have to track your revenue, your expenses, and your profit. After all, when you have a private practice, you really do have a business. And although you do not have to be a business guru, it is essential to know some basic business principles.

One of the most important business formulas to know is:

REVENUE – EXPENSES = PROFIT

There are a lot of ways to manipulate this equation to make a successful business. You can try to maximize revenue, control expenses carefully, or do some combination of the two in order to increase profits. That's why you must strategically decide on your path. Do you want to run your business like a Walmart or a Nordstrom? They are both successful businesses.

Walmart sells a lot of inexpensive widgets and makes a profit by keeping expenses low. However, that's not great for their employees' wages. Nordstrom, on the other hand, sells expensive products and is generally less worried about tight control of things like personnel expenses. Both of these approaches are equally valid and can yield profits.

The problem can occur if you don't watch both sides of the equation. It can look like you're doing great business, while at the same time you're headed for bankruptcy. This is why tracking is so vital.

Remember that there's more to business than volume. Having more clients does not guarantee more profit. You cannot just look at a busy business, whether it's a store, a restaurant, or a Registered Dietitian's office, and think that they are successful. You must know and understand the numbers. For instance, think about Groupon for restaurants. At first restaurant owners and customers alike loved Groupon. A lot of people bought coupons. But soon the restaurant owners realized that people buying the discounted coupons filled up the restaurant with much less profit than the regular customers. Even worse, because the restaurant was now filled with "cheaper" customers, it drove the regular, full paying customers away.

You may have experienced this in your own practice with insurance clients taking up prime appointment times, leaving no appointment times for regular clients who are paying full-price.

So even if your phone is ringing off the hook, your appointment books are packed, and client counseling rooms are full, how do you know whether your practice is making a profit? You must look at *all* the numbers.

WHAT TO TRACK

There are many things to measure so you can gauge the financial aspects of your business. When you follow your numbers, you can know how your business changes due to weather, holidays, and staff vacations. Additionally, your employees will respect what you take the time to inspect. Numbers do not lie; therefore, document and track your successes and encourage your team to do the same. Since most of your employees will be paid on commission, they will be inclined to help you track the numbers, as these numbers directly impact their earnings. Tracking and comparing to previous months and years is one of many valuable ways to quantify the financial health of your business. What tool do you use to track?

As a business owner, you must run reports to analyze the financial health of your business. These reports can be run each month, quarter, and year. Be sure to note any trends the numbers reveal. These numbers will help you forecast, set goals, and make important business decisions. The cash accounts must be reconciled to the monthly statements to ensure that the numbers are recorded correctly. Cash reconciliation gives the numbers credibility and enables you to discover and correct any errors or omissions.

REMEMBER: REVENUE – EXPENSES = PROFIT

Here are some ways to evaluate revenue or income, which is all the money coming into your business before you pay your bills.

- To analyze your reach to prospects, look at how your website and social media are doing.
    - Are people visiting your website?
    - How long are they staying?
    - What pages are they going to?
    - How many pages is each person viewing?
    - Which blogs are the most popular?
    - What are the Google Analytics of your website (more on this later)?
    - How many social media followers do you have?
    - Are they interacting with you online or just passive connections?
- To analyze client action and retention, look at your scheduling and EHR.
    - What is the number of new client appointments?
    - What is the number of follow-up appointments?
    - What is the number of programs/self-pay packages sold?
    - What is the number of referrals from each referral source?
    - What is the income based on various sources of revenue: self-pay clients, programs, insurance, classes, products?
    - What are the income trends based on each insurance company?

  - What is the income based on client diagnosis?
  - What is the number of appointments per Registered Dietitian?
  - What is the number of appointments scheduled by administrative staff?
  - How long does the average client stay with you?
  - What seasonal trends do you see? Are there more clients in the spring, after Thanksgiving, or in January?
  - Which days are busiest?

REMEMBER: REVENUE – EXPENSES = PROFIT

Here are some ways to analyze your expenses.

- To analyze your potential and current income, look at your money numbers.
  - Where is your money going?
  - What are your current expenses?
  - What are your forecasted expenses?
  - Do you have priorities spelled out?
  - Are your expenses in line with your values, mission statement, vision?
  - Do you have a budget?
  - Do you have profit goals?

REMEMBER: REVENUE – EXPENSES = PROFIT

Your profit is the revenue (income) minus the expenses. Trends in income and expenses determine trends in profit. Here are some ways to analyze your profit.

  - What is your profit/loss year to date?
  - What is your profit/loss compared to last year/last quarter?
  - Do all the numbers make sense? Are all the numbers explainable?

Again, busy does not guarantee success. It is important to think about revenue versus expenses. For example, if you are very busy and hire someone to help administratively, you might find that you're overstaffed at times … and there goes your profit.

Inspiration from Dana: "Being the newest addition to our Registered Dietitian team, I was in the salaried phase of our professional track for about nine months. Knowing the financial success Kait experienced upon making the switch to commissions, I was encouraged to track the revenue I brought into the business monthly to evaluate when I would be able to convert to commission-based pay. This helped me set goals to improve upon my numbers. Once I surpassed my hourly pay I was able to confidently switch to commissions."

Having this data at your fingertips is invaluable because you can see if you are making money versus losing money, growing in revenue or not, and answer many questions when trying to grow your business.

You can also use the information strategically to:

- Market your practice.
- Sell your practice and/or bring on a partner(s).
- Know when to hire new employees.
- Reach out to your top referrals.
- Capitalize on your most popular web pages.
- Attract clients based on their insurance or diagnosis. For example, RBA has one insurance company, Blue Cross Blue Shield for Federal Employees, which we learned through tracking will pay for six visits per year regardless of the diagnosis. This is such a strong marketing tool we can use to reach out to federal employees: "Six free nutrition visits per year."
- Discover who are the strongest Registered Dietitians for employee retention as well as your strongest staff members for employee appreciation.
- Identify which months, days, locations, and times are the busiest and slowest. By tracking this you can know if your Registered Dietitians should work unique hours, such as early mornings, late evenings, and even Saturdays, to take advantage of bringing in the greatest revenue. You can also schedule your administrative staff according to trends in new client calls.

If you are not passionate about the business side of your practice, find someone who can help you. To continue providing help to clients, you need to have a healthy business.

To help with the tracking, have regular meetings with your bookkeeper, biller, accountant, and attorney. You'll likely find that meeting with these professionals helps you stay focused and informed.

Inspiration from Dana: "It was a huge honor to be brought into my first meeting with RBA's bookkeeper, with whom our REBEL team meets with quarterly. I was exposed to the raw numbers behind the business and included in the analysis, interpretation, and policy creation from what the numbers were telling us. This meeting encourages us to keep striding forward, and the positive trends serve as motivation for continued outstanding performance."

Additionally, it is important to be able to learn the business lingo so you can speak intelligently to your business professionals, ask the right questions, and understand the information they tell you. Just because you are a REBEL, doesn't mean you can ignore the financial details of running a successful business. Therefore, read business books and magazines about marketing, selling, managing, running, and expanding a business.

Strive for structure and consistency in tracking your business. It's too easy for owners to fall behind in the financial aspects of the business. That's why getting help is essential. Just as clients need a strong treatment team, you need a team of professionals on your side. So use the experts, learn from them, and use their skills and tools to foster success.

And remember, track everything!

TRACKING YOUR REVENUE AND REFERRALS

Having a variety of revenue streams is essential for the strength and longevity of your business. As mentioned earlier, it is important to not rely on only one kind of counseling or one kind of client. It is best to have a variety of sources of income, such as self-pay individual counseling, insurance counseling, classes, groups, speaking, blogging, writing, books and products. That way, if your counseling hours decrease for whatever reason, you can generate income from another source.

These revenue streams seem to change over time. We have been involved with corporate classes, workshops, food sensitivity testing, measuring resting metabolic rates, protein/vitamin and mineral supplements, body composition measurements, and a variety of sources of revenue that seem to ebb and flow over time. No matter what revenue sources you choose, you need to always look at the numbers. You can follow your passion and use your intuition to a certain degree, but you must also look at numbers.

Aside from tracking client appointments, it is also important to know where these clients are coming from. Keep your eye on your referral sources (more on this later), so you know who are your top referring people. Make sure to keep those referral sources happy, and at the same time, cultivate new referral sources. For instance, if 80% of your referrals come from a certain physician, therapist, or insurance company, and that referral source dries up for any reason, then your business will decline. If you only make money by selling one thing or relying on one primary referral source, you are more vulnerable to dips in the economy. It is best to cast out a large net for potential business.

BILLING

Focusing on the money coming into your business is essential for private practice success. In addition to being a fantastic nutrition counselor, you need to have a good understanding of the financial details along the way. This enables you to make wise business decisions as you make changes to your business intentionally with as many facts as possible. Keeping a keen eye on the money is key. To better track the money coming into your business, consider billing in-house. RBA outsourced a biller at one time, which presented certain challenges such as:

- A delay in communication with billing insurance and clients
- A delay in posting payments

- Lack of availability to answer client questions
- Inconsistent monitoring of daily revenue
- Additional expense to pay an outside contractor

Because of the advances in technology, becoming your own biller has become significantly easier. It's something you want to seriously consider.

GETTING PAID FOR YOUR WORK: TAKING OWNERSHIP OVER YOUR BILLING AND EXPENSES

There is nothing more frustrating than providing client services and not getting paid because of billing incorrectly or as a result of an insurance denial. To ensure you get the money you deserve, keep the following points in mind:

- Safeguard your income with checks and balances for cash, checks, and credit card payments from collection to deposit.
- Know your insurance companies' rules, requirements, and reimbursement policies. These vary significantly and change often. You'll want to make sure your work is reimbursed, so follow the rules and develop policies to ensure consistency. You may find this frustrating at first, but be persistent for the sake of the client and for your revenue. Even if you decide to accept insurance, you can be a REBEL and be selective with the specific insurance companies that you choose to participate in.
- Run reports weekly with all outstanding monies owed to your business. This is called accounts receivable (AR). This money can be outstanding directly from the client (copay or deductible) or from insurance. For the Registered Dietitians on commission to be paid for their services covered by insurance, you will want to keep this number as low as possible. Take time each week to evaluate your AR or have an employee follow-up on all outstanding payments for 90 days or older, 60 days, and 30 days. Keep a detailed log of customer telephone calls, emails, and statements. Just as you would document all of your clients' clinical interventions, you want to be just as diligent with your paper trail concerning your clients' accounts.
- For outstanding balances such as copays, deductibles, or insurance denials, first contact the clients to make them aware of the situation. You may offer to accept payment over the phone by credit card, via Paypal, or by check through the mail.
- Set up a protocol for sending out statements to your clients. We suggest sending at least three statements over the course of three months requesting payment. A month after the last of these statements, give a courtesy call to the clients to warn them that their account

is delinquent and may be sent to collections. You will want to think long and hard before sending clients to collections, as there is a small likelihood you will actually get paid and it may lead to bad word of mouth. Also, there is a time limit on the opportunity to collect payment, and that if someone declares bankruptcy you may never get paid, BUT a small likelihood is often better than none!

- Sign up with a collections agency who will attempt to collect payment on your behalf. Realize that if the collections agency does receive payment they will keep a percentage of the bill. For this reason you may choose simply to offer a discount to clients for a prompt payment of their delinquent accounts, or you may want to write off low bills that would not generate much profit going through collections. You may also charge a collections fee to be added to the outstanding amount for this service. This must be clearly stated in your registration policies that clients have signed. Once an account has gone to collections you are no longer at liberty to settle or discuss the debt with the clients and all interaction must go through the collections agency. In the end, this is the professional route to take if you can find a company who aligns with your philosophies and who will not badger your clients.

Just as your clients will find blind spots in their nutrition, you may have blind spots in your billing. It is good to have an extra set of eyes to double check everything. Here are some things our accountant has brought to our attention:

- Whoever is printing checks to issue a refund or make bill payments should not be signing them. You as the business owner should approve all money leaving the business.
- As the business owner you should review the bank statement prior to reconciliation.
- Credit card receipts for all business purchases must be provided for all charges appearing on the statement(s). Again, attention to detail and making sure everything is documented with a clear paper trail is essential.
- Quarterly or semi-annually, an outside accountant should analyze the books to ensure that monthly reconciliations are performed properly. Journal entries and transaction deletions should be at a minimum, and all cash should be diligently managed and protected.
- Computer backup of all financials should be stored off-site (daily, weekly, or monthly depending on volume).

Inspiration from Rebecca: "Make sure you always have a plan B. I used to use an outside biller who was a victim of a natural disaster, causing us to be disconnected from our shared billing software and calendar for weeks. Without a backup plan, my team had to work hundreds of extra hours to re-enter her data into a new system in order to get the situation resolved."

ESTABLISH FINANCIAL GOALS

Most clients cringe when they hear the word "diet." Well, most Registered Dietitians in private practice cringe when they hear the word "budget." Both imply restrictions of some kind. Just as I don't want our clients dieting, I don't want our business restricted. Therefore, think of your budget as simply another way to set goals and reach your vision. Since our team has so much fun being REBELs, it can be a challenge for us to slow down and really look at the details. But when you use your budget as a planning tool, much like you would encourage your clients to plan their meals, you can experience great success.

One mistake made from the start was not regularly tracking revenue and expenses. As a result, the business didn't have concrete financial goals. Use your records and numbers to set up a budget to review monthly and quarterly so you can keep the data as consistent as possible. Having a budget will prepare you for as many expenses as you can so you are not caught unprepared. Setting financial goals can also help you plan for major expenses, such as a new computer, new office furniture, or a resting metabolic rate machine. It is also important to have enough wiggle room in the budget to be able to have resources to invest in something new like electronic health records or employee development.

As you create your rebellious budget, prioritize your expenses and start small. At first, you will be doing most things yourself to keep your practice afloat. As you grow, you will be able to add administrative staff or additional Registered Dietitians based on your priorities and your vision. Think of what is most important for you to invest in to grow your individual practice.

In terms of marketing, you don't need new business cards, brochures, a website, and a newsletter all at once. Instead, focus on creating one of these at a time. In terms of making sure that you have all the clinical tools you desire, do the same thing that you would do with your personal budget: Think about what you really need versus what would simply be nice to have. In other words, what would actually help you generate income versus just be something cool in the office? Looking at expected revenue and associated expenses will help you intelligently prioritize your business purchases.

Here's a great tip: Start a wish list that you can revisit at future budget meetings and act on when applicable. Remember, you have to spend money to make money as you start dreaming big and converting your solo practice into a larger business.

Your budget may be completely different, but here is an example of some of our budget expense categories:

EMPLOYEES

- Payroll expenses
- Health insurance
- Retirement accounts
- Workers compensation
- Electronic Health Records
- Tablets
- Professional development
- Reference materials
- Professional liability expenses
- Uniforms
- Automobile expenses
- Employee appreciation
- Meals and entertainment
- Travel
- Dues and subscriptions
- Dietetic Practice Group subscriptions

ADVERTISING AND PROMOTION

- Website
- Referral listing websites
- Brochures
- Business cards

OFFICE MAINTENANCE

- Rent/mortgage
- Utilities
- Repair/maintenance
- Internet
- Telephone
- Furniture
- Office equipment (scale, resting metabolic rate machines, body fat analysis, blood pressure cuffs)
- Office supplies
- Postage and delivery
- Cleaning service
- Shredding company

BUSINESS EXPENSES

- Bank service charges
- Credit card expenses
- Business licenses and permits
- Taxes
- Depreciation expenses

Preparing these numbers takes a lot of time, and this is where you may want to hire someone outside the business to work through your numbers. It also helps to have an unbiased source looking at your bottom line, rather than getting caught up in the day-to-day numbers. Although you might not be preparing all the numbers, it is important for you to understand them and be prepared to ask essential questions to better interpret your day-to-day business and trends.

Inspiration from Rebecca "Even though I have learned much about keeping my eye on the books and improving the overall health of the business, the reality is that I get much more excited about counseling clients and empowering my Registered Dietitians—that it is difficult for me to stay on top of all the numbers of the business. Over the past year, I have put into place a system where I meet with my accountant monthly to go over all the business numbers and quarterly with my REBEL business team."

REBEL SUCCESS STRATEGIES

ASSIGNMENTS

☐ Make a list of all your expenses to help you keep track of your finances.

____

____

____

____

____

____

____

____

____

- [ ] Set up a spreadsheet to help you track the monthly client and financial numbers:
    - Number of new appointments
    - Number of follow-up appointments
    - Number of programs/self-pay packages sold
    - Number of referrals from each referral source
    - Number of hits on your website and the most popular pages
    - Number of social media followers
    - Income based on revenue stream, clients, insurance, classes, products
    - Income based on each insurance company
    - Income based on client diagnosis
    - The number of appointments per Registered Dietitian
    - The number of appointments booked per administrative staff

- [ ] Use this information to create a budget. Prioritize what you need now versus what you want. Consider hiring a bookkeeper to help you get started. You will need receipts and expenses from the prior years. Remember, if you're investing hours into performing and managing the accounting needs of your business, you're losing valuable hours that you should be using to manage and grow your business, which is your true passion. Hire the experts to manage the accounting tasks that are their specialty so you can invest your time and energy in your passion: counseling clients.

"By failing to prepare, you are preparing to fail."

– Benjamin Franklin

REBEL RD

CHAPTER SIX

R – Reach New Heights

Grow Your Business Through Strategic Marketing

Marketing is one of the exciting and creative aspects of what we do outside of counseling our clients. Rebecca, Dana, and I love spreading our rebellion and empowering people, both personally and professionally. We encourage you to think about marketing your practice in a new way. What do you want to convey to your audience (your current and potential clients)? Think back to the beginning of this workbook and look at your strengths and your passion. What is important to YOU? That is the best place to start. You can then think about how best to help and reach others.

RBA's reach has grown exponentially with our continued efforts in various marketing platforms. I hope this chapter inspires you to utilize new and interesting forms of marketing for your business. Think about marketing as simply connecting. Who, what, when, why, and how will you find and nurture current and future referral sources and clients? You can market yourself to individuals (potential clients) or influencers (potential referral sources).

Marketing can even include providing services above and beyond expectations. Never underestimate the value of word-of-mouth marketing, which will reach influencers who see many potential clients each day. In addition, set a schedule for yourself to intentionally target health professionals based on your niche. These include physicians in family medicine, internal medicine, endocrinology, pediatrics, or obstetrics and gynecology. Think outside of the box to include dentists, therapists, pastors, professors, corporations, philanthropic organizations, professional organizations, and anyone who values and appreciates wellness! Focus on how your services can help other professionals save time and money, and foster greater success of their clients.

REACHING OUT TO HEALTHCARE PROFESSIONALS

- Physician Office Mailings: Physicians are an excellent source of referrals. They often have a vast amount of clients and minimal time to spend talking about weight, nutrition, and food choices. Having a strong nutrition source to refer to helps strengthen their practice with happy and healthy clients. Set a goal, such as ten mailings every week, until you've contacted all the physicians in your immediate area. Include in the mailing either an introduction letter of how you can help their clients or gratitude for referrals and support, brochures, business cards, prescription pads, and flyers with any new services or programs.
- Visiting Physicians' Offices: Visiting physicians' offices is another way to market to the influencer. Be prepared to not always get a meeting. Calling ahead can help but the physician may not always be free at the scheduled time. You should set a goal of visiting at least one physician office each month. Here are some tips for visiting physician offices:
  - Call the receptionist to set up a loose time frame one week before visiting.
  - Have a five-minute speech prepared to give the physicians about what you can offer their clients and how you can help both their clients and the physician be more successful.
  - Have brochures, business cards, or referral pads to leave in the office. Referral pads make it very easy for the physician and the client to get in touch with you. Remember, you may not be able to have all of these marketing tools at the beginning, but you can set goals to add one new tool each year.
  - Be sure to communicate that you will keep their practice in mind for clients needing a physician.
  - You may want to consider bringing a small gift for the receptionist and office staff to make a memorable impression, such as a small gift basket of fruit, a pound of coffee, or a candle.
  - Bring work with you. You may have to sit in a certain office for an hour or more; always have things to do so you don't miss out on a day of productivity.
  - Follow up two to three days later with a thank you note or call the office and thank the staff!

Ideas for Connecting with Other Healthcare Professionals

- Meet therapists for coffee.
- Visit treatment centers.
- Call community centers and schools.
- Attend local Registered Dietitian networking events.

Inspiration from Rebecca: "Personal connections are priceless. Take the time to meet or call your referral sources. The doctor's office staff loves to be able to put a name to a face, so it is worth the effort to set up meetings with the office managers, physicians, and other medical staff."

COMMUNICATIONS WITH PHYSICIANS OR CLIENTS WHO REFER

Make it a priority to send out a report of your intervention to your clients' health professionals. You can mail a report to the physician with your business cards, brochures, and prescription pads or send a fax with a "Thanks for your referral" note handwritten on the page. This will keep you at the front of their minds for referral opportunities.

It is also wise to think of another time of the year to appreciate those who refer to you. You can send online "e-cards" during the holidays, offer to do a National Nutrition Month activity in their office, or even send a handwritten note thanking them for their referrals. Rather than sending holiday cards when most people do, consider sending Thanksgiving Cards or Valentines Cards (We Love Your Referrals!).

OPEN HOUSE

You may choose to host an open house at your office yearly. You can invite clients, potential clients, and local health professionals to attend and to host a table promoting their services if desired. This can be a great way to network with other professionals and to attract new referral sources.

MARKETING MATERIALS

The following are some marketing ideas to consider. While this is not an all-inclusive list, it will give you some inspiration to get started. If you want to learn more about marketing, invest in some marketing books and seek out advice from marketing professionals.

- **Brochures:**
  First, know that brochures can come at a large expense. You may need to hire a graphic designer to make your vision come to life. You will also have printing costs for the brochure. Decide if you want brochures for your business, programs, or both. You will want to develop the branding for your program first and then emulate that theme with your brochure. Make sure your brochure focuses on the challenges of your clients, then how your program will help conquer these struggles, and then about you. Include a strong call to action and information about how to contact you, such as your website and social media links. Finally, be mindful of how you use these brochures to market your business. Will they go out to referring providers upon request? Will you send them out to providers in your area? Will you visit community groups and organizations?

Examples of our marketing materials: brochures for our RBA company as well as our individual nutrition programs and referral pads we provide for our referring physicians.

Inspiration from Dana: "My experience creating the REBEL Dieting Program brochure with our graphic designer was long and tedious, but the end result was well worth it. Don't settle for something that is just okay; aim for excellence. Marketing materials are costly and should be exactly what you want. It is important to boldly convey your branding appropriately for your programs or business in order to have a strong presence among all of the nutrition and dieting programs receiving attention out there. For the REBEL Dieting Program, I wanted to make something different that stood out from the crowd and spoke to anyone who picked up our brochure that they too could be part of the REBELLION against diets."

- **Business cards:**
  As an entrepreneur and as a counseling Registered Dietitian, you need to have business cards with you at all times. As I mentioned earlier, everyone you meet is a potential client or referral source. Be sure to make your business cards easy to read and unique in some way.

Our team has found it is helpful to have a picture of our Registered Dietitians on the cards to put a face with the name and make them stand out. You may also want to list your social media links and website.

- **Postcards:**
  This is a less expensive way to market your business, programs, or Registered Dietitians. Much like brochures, postcards should contribute to the marketing of your program with what challenges you will help your clients face, how you will help them do this, and then information about you.

- **Thank you notes:**
  Show your gratitude by sending handwritten thank you notes whenever possible. It will make a lasting impression. You can send them to staff, students, volunteers/interns, referring providers, or other Registered Dietitians.

- **Bulletin Boards:**
  Take advantage of your space to highlight your business, programs, and staff. Depending on space, feature one person per month or all of your employees with information about them professionally and personally. This will help with likability and relatability to your clients. It will also help create buzz and get people engaged.

For examples of our marketing materials, please visit our website at www.rbitzer.com.

Examples of our bulletin boards that are hung in our main lobby and individual offices. We use these to provide information about our programs and inspire our clients.

HOW TO GROW YOUR PRACTICE WITH SOCIAL MEDIA

I believe that the future of our profession relies heavily on being able to keep up with the unbelievable power and potential of social media. Take advantage of your resources and empower your student interns (who are typically experts in social media) to build upon their strengths to create a win-win situation. Encourage them to start creating a name for themselves in social media and strengthen the future of dietetics while helping you to promote your business, Registered Dietitians, and programs. Be a part of the conversation and get out there where potential clients, referral sources, and your peers are.

An increasingly valuable way to market your practice is through social media. However, you have to keep in mind how much time you are spending on social media and track trends to see what is successful and what is a waste of time and energy. Create a company blog, Facebook page, Twitter handle, Pinterest board, Instagram page, and whatever else becomes popular as time evolves. Use these accounts to provide inspirational content, establish yourself as a professional, and ultimately drive people to your website.

Inspiration from Rebecca: "Using technology is an introvert's paradise. I can quickly and easily connect to others using email, texting, blogging, Facebook, LinkedIn, Twitter and more without ever having to say a word. I especially love the efficiency of these adventures because I feel like I can make ten times more initial connections and then follow up in person or on the phone."

THE FIRST STEP TO SOCIAL MEDIA SUCCESS: GET ORGANIZED

As you plan your social media activities, keep the following points in mind:

- What do you want your mission to be? What take-away do you want your clients, referral sources, and other health professionals to leave with when they visit your social media sites? Make sure your posts all come back to that main idea.
- Start by outlining monthly themes that will help organize your social media postings. Some examples include Heart Health Month, Digestive Health Month, and Love Your Body Month. Also, be sure to include program launches and events in your area. Get creative!
- Get some consistency and buzz going on all of your social media pages that can be shared by other websites. Make sure to focus on your particular area of work and pick themes that represent your niche.

- Think about which social media your clients use; if you don't know, then ask!
- Once you have your themes and ideas laid out on paper, set a social media strategy for posting on these various outlets.
- It can be challenging to manage a variety of different social media sources. There are sites such as Hootsuite (www.hootsuite.com) that will link multiple social media sites in order for you to schedule postings with links in advance, all in one place.
- Be sure to track the number of hits on your website, the most popular pages that people visit, and the number of social media followers you have.

"Until you consistently review analytics, you'll never know which components of your social media strategy are and aren't working." – David Nour, writing in InformationWeek

YOUR WEBSITE

Your website is your gateway to attracting new clients, supporting your current clients, networking with other professionals, and selling your services. The quality of your website and the ease in which it can be accessed directly impact your credibility in your profession. You can spend thousands of dollars on your website, but we recommend you grow your site as you grow your business.

Your website should include the following items:

- Contact information, including your address, email, phone numbers, and fax number (front and center)
- The ability to easily make an appointment or request more information
- Biographies of your Registered Dietitians and information about their specialties
- Information about your programs
- Your blog postings
- Option to subscribe to your newsletter
- Testimonials
- Products you may be selling
- Twitter, Pinterest, Facebook, and other social media links

Visit www.rbitzer.com to see the content on our website.

BLOGGING

Blogging is the most important social media outlet because it has the longest lifespan, it comes up when searching on search engines, and you can create handouts from your top blogs. Your Registered Dietitians can blog on their specialty, which then leads back to your company's main website. Other considerations for your blog include:

- Make a blog schedule featuring one to three posts per week (depending on where you are starting). Assign topics based on your social media monthly themes to both Registered Dietitians and students. Rotate topics such as recipes, motivational inspirations, nutrition in the news, successful clients, company highlights, and events. Post consistently on the same days each week and around the same time, and remember to keep your overall mission in mind. Blogs should be informal conversations that provoke interaction with your audience. Be sure to ask questions or for feedback at the end of your posts to help generate comments.
- Hyperlink to pages on your website or other resources, but always have these pages open in a new tab or window so visitors are not taken away from your site.
- Feature interviews with successful clients on your blog. It is wonderful for clients to share their success and it also acts as free marketing.
- Post a monthly feature of your favorite blogs from around the web. Highlighting other sites and professionals on your blog will allow for greater sharing opportunities from these featured writers. To easily keep track of your favorite blogs, set up an organizational website, such as Feedly, to collect the blogs you follow.
- Develop consistent blog topics that relate to your nutrition niche that clients look forward to reading. Some of our blog themes include:
    - ☑ Meal Planning, Not Perfection
    - ☑ Sunday Meal Prep
    - ☑ What It's Like Living With a REBEL Dietitian
    - ☑ Step-by-Step Meal Prep
    - ☑ From the Registered Dietitian's Table: Lunch Break at our Nutrition Office
    - ☑ Motivational Monday (success stories and positive testimonials from our clients)
    - ☑ From College Girl to College Girl (Rebelling Against Dieting on Campus)

- Reach out to companies for products, food samples, materials, or anything you think may be of interest to your readers. Offer companies a review in exchange for samples that you can use as giveaways to clients to increase readership for your blog.
- Track your most popular blogs and keep these post topics in mind for the future.
- Post all your blogs to your other social media outlets.
- Images associated with blogs that appear on your site and marketing materials will make strong impressions. Make sure they look professional. Take a photography class or a class at your local Apple store to improve your skills with capturing and utilizing photos in all your networks and branding across all print and social media platforms. If this is neither a strength nor an interest of yours, then hire a photographer for headshots or other promotional materials rather than use a camera phone to meet your needs. In terms of using images found online, only use images that permit copying depending on the license. The Academy of Nutrition and Dietetics has a few free resources you can use at: http://www.eatright.org/Members. Or you can use Google Image search: http://www.google.com/imghp.

    Follow the directions below:

    1. Type in your search term and hit enter.
    2. Click on the Search Tools button to view another menu.
    3. Use the Usage Rights dropdown to select "Labeled for Reuse."

    Flickr has a similar search function to ensure you aren't using any copyrighted images without permission. If you find something on the web that you want to use and you are unsure about the copyright, your best bet is to contact the person or organization who posted it and ask their permission.
- Use as many professional photos as possible, but it is also fun to use simple snapshots of your everyday life, including food, self-care, or your interests, in your blog or social media posts. This can help your clients identify you as a real person and shatter the nutritional perfectionism stigma of a Registered Dietitian.

NEWSLETTERS

Regularly scheduled email newsletters are a great way to give back to your clients with fun tips, recipes, and inspirational quotes. It can also be used to highlight new blog posts, what you are doing as a company, or any upcoming local events. Try not to be salesy and rather use it as a way to give back to your community, share information, and provide value. Once you have a template designed, empower a student to fulfill the task of creating the weekly or monthly newsletter. Add clients, colleagues, family, friends, and acquaintances to your newsletter subscription to broaden your reach. Newsletters are likely to go viral, and they are a good way to repurpose your blogs and other information.

TWITTER

Twitter is an online microblogging service that allows you to connect with your followers using short, 140 character "tweets." This makes it ideal for people who have limited time to peruse social media, as they can still gather interesting and useful messages from your company via Twitter. Use Twitter to network, attract business leads, and follow relevant conversations in your industry. Additional considerations include:

- Make of list of hashtags to use in your tweets that will link up with other professional Twitter accounts in your field. A hashtag is defined as a word or phrase preceded by a hash or pound sign (#) and used to identify messages on a specific topic.
- Search keywords in Twitter to find influencers in nutrition, health, and business to follow and get yourself known in your industry of choice. Be wise with whom you follow. To be considered a leader in the Twitter world you need to be selective in who you follow. To become one of these influencers yourself, it is not about who you follow but who follows you.
- Engage in Twitter chats hosted by colleagues in your field.
- Keep track of your followers, comments, favorited tweets, and re-tweets.
- Just as you are hoping to have other Registered Dietitians and readers "share" and "retweet" your posts, make sure you do the same for them! "Retweet" and "Favorite" tweets from other Registered Dietitians and health professionals to keep the conversation going.

FACEBOOK

You can use Facebook to build a community to engage former and current clients and attract new clients. Facebook is a way to provide daily support, information, and inspiration for clients of varying demographics. It is wise to develop a Facebook page for your company, separate from your personal timeline, where you offer unique tools for connecting people to a topic they care about. Other points about Facebook include:

- Schedule your posts to fit your monthly or weekly theme.
- Use Facebook for promotions, giveaways, and announcements.

- Create photo albums to document recipes and events.
- You may use Facebook to encourage donating to a charity that is important to your business to give back. For example, you may pledge to donate a certain amount of money or food per like on Facebook.
- Keep track of which Facebook posts get the most likes and shares.
- Facebook is a casual, friendly way for clients to get to know you and trust you.

Inspiration from Rebecca: "Think about your social media as a way to give current and potential clients a tiny spoonful of your wealth of knowledge and value, just like when the person at the ice cream counter gives you a tiny taste of ice cream before you decide which ice cream cone to buy. Remember how sales are made: know, like, try, trust, then buy."

LINKEDIN

Think of LinkedIn as way to reach more influencers and endorse professionals to grow our profession. Key points about LinkedIn include:

- Join groups on LinkedIn relevant to your field to meet other health professionals.
- Keep your eye on business trends on LinkedIn.
- Write recommendations for your administrative students and Registered Dietitians to give back and help grow their career.
- Further your credibility by keeping an up-to-date resume.
- Post articles of interest to your Linkedin subscribers.

PINTEREST

Pinterest is perfect for Registered Dietitians because food is very visual. Make sure all your blogs have high quality pictures that can easily be added to your Pinterest boards. Additional considerations include:

- Create a board for each of your Registered Dietitians and specialties.
- Think outside the box. Create boards for self-care, quotes that are applicable to your clients, and anything else that can have a strong visual appeal.

Inspiration from Rebecca: "I was a skeptic of Pinterest at first, but Kait's boards have actually brought clients into our office. Who would have thought that online 'scrapbooking' would have been such a hit?"

YOUTUBE

Think of videos as a way to "blog" using a video camera or by simply recording on your webcam. You may create a series of videos based on one central theme or based on your social media schedule for the month. Go with your strengths. If you are uncomfortable on camera this may be a task for your student administrative team. YouTube videos are another great way to showcase corporate wellness or educational talks if you have a few edited clips that can be placed on your website. Videos tap into your audience's senses and are another way for the reader to get to know you. Again, bring everything back to your theme and get creative. For example, we have recorded various video series, such as "Mindful Minutes," What REBELs Eat," and "Quick Nutrition Tips."

YouTube is the second most used search engine, behind Google; therefore, label your videos with keywords so they are searchable.

Inspiration from Rebecca: "Keep your eyes out for up and coming forms of social media. There are currently so many social media platforms that it can be overwhelming to get started. But just like most things, start small with one form of social media and get good at it before you start learning a second form of social media. Over time you will see which forms of social media are most effective for your practice."

BE A STAR: GET YOUR NAME OUT THERE

One of the great things about marketing is that it is always evolving. As new mediums launch and as client preferences change, you'll want to change your marketing efforts accordingly. On the surface this can seem intimidating, but it really allows you to unleash your creativity, set yourself apart from the crowd, and become known as the dietetic practice of choice. As you continually fine-tune and update your marketing messages, keep these final points in mind:

- Contact both local and national media sources to submit articles and web content. Websites are always looking for credible nutrition content to fill up space. Although you may not be directly financially compensated, getting your name out in your community will get you visibility to your potential clients. For example, I write articles for the Washingtonian online health section, WTOP news station in DC, and STACK Media (sports nutrition website) where people can click back to my personal and company website.
- Your audience will enjoy reading reviews of your services before purchasing. Make sure your happy, successful clients take the time to give you five stars on any forum that reviews services, such as Angie's List, Health Grades, or Yelp.
- RBA enjoys featuring our client successes every Monday on our blog and Facebook with Motivational Monday. What a great way to start the week!
- Have your student Google your name and other keywords such as your location and specialty to track your visibility on the internet. It will increase your rankings on Google by searching your own name or company name on a regular basis.
- Be where your clients are. Set up listings on the Academy of Nutrition and Dietetics (AND), Sports, Cardiovascular and Wellness Nutrition (SCAN), National Eating Disorder Association (NEDA), your local Dietetic Practice Group (DPG), and other referral sites.

REBEL SUCCESS STRATEGIES

ASSIGNMENTS

- [ ] Make a list of all the professionals you need to meet with in your area. Create a "to-do" item on your calendar to visit each of these referral sources over the next year.

____

____

____

____

☐ What are some themes for your social media postings? Keep in mind your niche and ideal client to focus posts, and then create a schedule for posting.

☐ Commit to posting blogs one time per week based on your theme.

☐ Google your name, as well as nutrition services in your area, and see how you are listed on these sites. Also check out your client review pages to see how you are rated.

"I've found that luck is quite predictable. If you want more luck, take more chances. Be more active. Show up more often."

– Brian Tracy

REBEL RD

CHAPTER SEVEN

D – Dare to Be a REBEL

Be a Registered Dietitian AND a Business Owner

As you can see, every aspect of my professional life is a bit untraditional and rebellious.

I WAS A REBEL INTERN WHEN I WAS...

- Working with Registered Dietitians in varying fields to find my passion, align my strengths, and search for my perfect career.
- Keeping up with technology trends and being innovative in my work opportunities.
- Seeking out all the job experiences I could and embracing the take-away even of those that were not my favorite.
- Never being comfortable and always searching for the next opportunity.
- Seeking out new projects and ways to get involved instead of letting them come to me.

I AM A REBEL DIETITIAN WHEN I AM...

- Helping clients resist diets, live joyfully, and develop a positive relationship with food.
- Supporting clients while they incorporate foods they love.
- Communicating with the clients in my program daily.
- Working with clients in my specialty and referring out to other health professionals for clients who need a higher level of care or instances outside of my specialty.

I AM A REBEL BUSINESSWOMAN WHEN I AM...

- Building my client base by traveling to physicians' offices, cold-calling health professionals, and branding myself on social media.
- Taking a risk by switching to commission and doubling my income.
- Creating self-pay programs that create both client growth and personal happiness.
- Exploring new technologies to support our practice.

I INSPIRE FUTURE REBEL DIETITIANS IN NUTRITION AND BUSINESS WHEN I AM...

- Paving the way for future interns to be hired into successful private practices.
- Training dietetic students on nutrition, preparing them for their dietetic internship, and sharing cutting edge nutrition and business success principles.
- Helping private practice Registered Dietitians create unlimited earning potential in the nutrition counseling practice of their dreams.
- Coaching Registered Dietitians on how to implement successful programs with their clients.

WHY SHOULD YOU DARE TO REBEL?

As a REBEL Dietitian you will...

- **R** – Realize your potential by creating a fulfilling practice where you are able to do what you love and earn what you deserve.
- **E** – Excel in your niche where you have focused your energy.
- **B** – Build your private practice to unleash your vision, which might include hiring employees /and or expanding locations.
- **E** – Empower your clients to be successful and happy.
- **L** – Learn ways to continually keep your practices financially successful.
- **R** – Reach new heights.
- **D** – Dare to be a REBEL.

WHY YOU WILL LOVE BEING A REBEL

Imagine working in your dream job, being part of a team of like-minded REBELs who never fail to amaze you, and interacting with clients who inspire you as much as you inspire them. Imagine earning income you never thought possible and having a flexible schedule. Imagine living a balanced life that allows you plenty of time for what matters most to you, whether it's family, friends, hobbies, self-care, and/or community involvement. Imagine having a career that's an extension of your personal life. All that and more is possible! You simply need to REBEL to make it happen.

Being a REBEL Dietitian is so much more than basic Registered Dietitian training. It is about self-learning and continued growth, recognizing and aligning your strengths, networking and positioning yourself as the expert, and having the business savvy to support the work you love.

HOW TO BE A REBEL DIETITIAN

- Commit your time to completing all the activities in this workbook. They have lead RBA to where it is today, and we have no doubt these steps will strengthen your business.
- Follow our Facebook page, Welcome to the REBELution at facebook.com/REBELRD, to find entrepreneurial nutrition resources and tips.
- Sign up for our newsletter at www.rbitzer.com.
- Follow our blog for business case studies.
- Contact us at admin@rbitzer.com to find our hidden page on our website for more information about what you have found in this workbook.
- Contact us for business coaching to take your practice to the next level!

"Expect problems and eat them for breakfast."

– Alfred E. Montapert

RECOMMENDED READING

BUSINESS RESOURCES:

7 Habits of Highly Effective People: Powerful Lessons in Personal Change by Stephen R. Covey. DC Books, 2005.

Book Yourself Solid: The Fastest, Easiest, and Most Reliable System for Getting More Clients Than You Can Handle Even if You Hate Marketing and Selling by Michael Port. Wiley, 2010.

Built to Sell: Creating a Business that Can Thrive Without You by John Warrillow. Penguin Group, 2011.

The Compound Effect: Jumpstart Your Income, Your Life, Your Success by Darren Hardy. Vanguard Press, 2011.

Delivering Happiness: A Path to Profits, Passion, and Purpose by Tony Hsieh. Business Plus, 2010.

The E-Myth Revisited: Why Most Small Businesses Don't Work and What You Can Do About It by Michael E Gerber. HarperCollins Publishers, 2009.

Eat That Frog: 21 Great Ways to Stop Procrastinating and Get More Done in Less Time by Brian Tracy. Berrett-Koehler Publishers, 2007.

EntreLeadership: 20 Years of Practical Business Wisdom from the Trenches by Dave Ramsey. Howard Books, 2011.

Good to Great: Why Some Companies Make the Leap … And Others Don't by Jim Collins.HarperBusiness, 2011.

Independent Contractor (Self-Employed) or Employee? IRS Publication. www.irs.gov/Businesses/Small-Businesses-&-Self-Employed/Independent-Contractor-Self-Employed-or-Employee.

Lean In: Women, Work, and the Will to Lead by Sheryl Sandberg. Random House, 2013.

The Psychology of Selling: Increase Your Sales Faster and Easier Than You Ever Thought Possible by Brian Tracy. HarperCollins, 2005.

Success Magazine

The Success Principles: How to Get from Where You Are to Where You Want to Be by Jack Canfield. HarperCollins, 2009.

Think and Grow Rich by Napoleon Hill. Ballantine Books, 1988.

Women & Money: Owning the Power to Control Your Destiny by Suze Orman. Spiegel & Grau, 2007.

COUNSELING RESOURCES:

Counseling Tips for Nutrition Therapists Practice Workbook, volumes 1 and 2, by Molly Kellogg, RD, LCSW. Kg Press, 2006.

Intuitive Eating: A Revolutionary Program that Works by Evelyn Tribole, MS, RD and Elyse Resch, MS, RD, FADA. St. Martin's Griffin (Third Edition), 2012.

HEALTH CARE RESOURCES:

Electronic Health Records Information: www.officeally.com

HIPAA Information: www.hhs.gov/ocr/privacy/

NUTRITION/ REGISTERED DIETITIAN RESOURCES:

Academy of Nutrition and Dietetics: www.eatright.org

All Access Internships: Get Matched by Jenny Westerkamp, RD. www.allaccessinternships.com/GettingMatched.AGuideforDieteticsStudents.pdf

The Competitive Edge: Advanced Marketing for Dietetics Professionals (Third Edition) by Kathy King. Lippincott Williams & Wilkins, 2012.

The Entrepreneurial Nutritionist (Fourth Edition) by Kathy King. Lippincott Williams & Wilkins, 2009.

Just Jump: The No-Fear Business Start-Up Guide for Health and Fitness Professionals by Marjorie Geiser. California Based Publishing, 2011.

Making Nutrition Your Business: Private Practice and Beyond by Faye Berger Mitchell, RD and Ann M. Silver, MS, RD, CDE, CDN. American Dietetic Association, 2010.

Nutrition Entrepreneur Dietetic Practice Group: www.nedpg.org/

SELF-AWARENESS RESOURCES:

Essentials of Myers-Briggs Type Indicator® Assessment (Essentials of Psychological Assessment) by Naomi L. Quenk, PhD. Wiley, 2009.

Please Understand Me: Character & Temperament Types by David Keirsey and Marilyn Bates. B&D Books, 1984.

StrengthsFinder 2.0 by Tom Rath. Gallup Press, 2013.

What Are Your Values? Deciding What's Most Important In Life (Mind Tools Website). www.mindtools.com/pages/article/newTED_85.htm

SELF-CARE RESOURCES:

The Happiness Trap: How to Stop Struggling and Start Living by Russ Harris. Shambhala, 2014.

Having Your All: How Self-Care Leads to an Energized, Empowered, and Effective Life by Emma Fogt, MBA, MS, RDN and Nisha Shah, MPH, RDN. eWomen Wellness, 2014.

Nice Girls Don't Get the Corner Office: 101 Unconscious Mistakes Women Make That Sabotage Their Careers by Lois P Frankel, Ph.D. Business Plus, 2010.

Organize your Office In No Time by Monica Ricci. Que Publishing, 2005.

KAIT FORTUNATO GREENBERG, RD, LD

Kait Fortunato Greenberg is a Registered Dietitian in private practice at Rebecca Bitzer and Associates (RBA). Kait works with the non-dieting approach to intuitive eating, working with clients to form a healthy relationship with food. Kait and colleague Dana Magee launched the REBEL Dieting Program to further this message. She empowers her REBEL clients to eat mindfully and live joyfully while nourishing the body with a balance between health and enjoyment. She is an expert meal planner and helps individual clients and families prioritize health and self-care. She works hard to spread the non-dieting message on social media, encouraging people to not let food get in the way of what truly matters in their life and to start loving themselves for who they are. She is an active blogger spreading this message to thousands of readers via rebel-dietitian.com, rbitzer.com, wtop.com, washingtonian.com, and stackmedia.com.

Aside from excelling in nutrition therapy and counseling, Kait is very passionate about helping Registered Dietitians and nutrition interns. She started as a volunteer at RBA in 2009 and eventually was hired as a full-time Registered Dietitian, and she wanted to pave the way for future students to do the same. As such, she launched a mentorship track at RBA to provide college students experience in private practice. This continues to help successful volunteers be promoted to paid student interns and to gain valuable experience to obtain an accredited dietetic internship by the Academy of Nutrition and Dietetics. She is passionate about helping colleagues in the field REBEL against traditional norms of the dietetics workforce and to earn what they deserve while doing what they love. She also makes sure to stay involved in the dietetics field and give back to the profession. Kait was named the Outstanding Young Registered Dietitian of the Year in 2013 by the Academy of Nutrition and Dietetics Practice and is an active member of the Sports, Cardiovascular, and Wellness Nutrition (SCAN) dietetic practice group and the District of Columbia Metro Area Dietetic Association (DCMADA).

Kait feels fortunate to have been mentored by Rebecca Bitzer both in business and counseling skills, and wants to pay it forward. With business savvy and drive, Kait learned to work smarter and double her income in her second year of private practice. She offers business coaching for Registered Dietitians, helping to push them out of their comfort zone to take risks and share what she has learned along the way. Kait is a firm believer that everything happens for a reason, making sure to stay positive and practice gratitude while embracing each opportunity. She wants to help you do the same.

REBECCA BITZER, MS, RD, LD, CEDRD

Rebecca Bitzer is the founder of Rebecca Bitzer & Associates (RBA), an award-winning private practice group. As a pioneer in private practice since 1989, Rebecca has successfully developed and implemented innovative individual and group nutrition counseling programs. Rebecca has grown her practice through her uncanny ability to combine nutrition knowledge, counseling skills, and business savvy. Presently, Rebecca oversees multiple locations, 13 employees, 7,000 appointments per year, and 7 hand-selected, excellent Registered Dietitians.

Rebecca has written numerous published articles, co-authored a textbook chapter on Medical Nutrition Therapy, and has been featured in both nutrition and business textbooks. She is a former board member of Nutrition Entrepreneurs, a Dietetic Practice Group of the Academy of Nutrition and Dietetics, and will begin teaching a business/nutrition counseling course at University of Maryland in the spring of 2015. She earned her Master's degree from the University of Maryland in Food and Nutrition and completed her dietetic internship at the University of Virginia Medical Center in Charlottesville, Virginia.

Rebecca launched the Empowered Eating program, designed to provide hope for people and their loved ones who struggle with eating disorders. As one of the few Certified Eating Disorder Registered Dietitians (CEDRD) in the country, Rebecca has received additional formal education and training along with hands-on experience helping hundreds of clients improve their health using sound nutrition principles specifically tailored to mental illness and severe, potentially life-threatening medical complications caused by or associated with eating disorders.

As a business coach, Rebecca has successfully mentored other Registered Dietitians and health professionals to take their businesses to the next level. Rebecca uses her unique style of creative thinking and ability to inspire talented people to make their dreams a reality.

DANA MAGEE, RD, LD

Dana Magee is the most recent addition to the team of Registered Dietitians at Rebecca Bitzer & Associates (RBA). She started working with the company while earning her Bachelor of Science degree in Dietetics from the University of Maryland and returned to RBA after graduating from her dietetic internship with ARAMARK.

Within one year she fast-tracked her experience as a nutrition counselor with over 250 clients under her care. She was also charged with managing the main office and student interns along the mentorship track. She became the direct link for communication between the Registered Dietitians and the administrative team. Other milestones achieved during her first year include leading the complete switch of the whole practice to electronic health records, revamping billing and office procedures for efficiency and optimal communication, publishing a book on growing a private practice, and presenting over 20 nutrition seminars throughout the community for clients as well as to nutrition and health professionals.

One of her proudest accomplishments has been developing the REBEL Dieting Program, from the ground up with fellow RBA Registered Dietitian, Kait Fortunato Greenberg. The REBEL Dieting Program incorporates frequent individual nutrition counseling sessions combined with 24/7 email and text support to rebuild clients' relationship with food and steer clear of the next dieting disappointment that ultimately leaves them further away from their health goals. This program is set up to improve upon the client's nutrition knowledge, better their quality of life, and conquer emotional eating or binge eating.

Through speaking and individual nutrition counseling, Dana's passion for supporting her clients with the tools they need to achieve excellent nutrition shines. She guides her clients to become experts on their own nutritional needs and works alongside them to get them the long-term results they are seeking.

Dana also has a passion for creating quick and easy dishes as well as trying new recipes and sharing them with her clients. She further supports her clients with a blog and Facebook page dedicated to nutritional resources as well as step-by-step food preparation and grocery shopping tips.

Dana can help you make the transition from student to intern to Registered Dietitian to REBEL Dietitian in business.

ABOUT REBECCA BITZER & ASSOCIATES

OUR MISSION:

The mission of Rebecca Bitzer MS, RD & Associates, Inc: The Nutrition Experts is to provide our clients with sound, evidenced-based nutrition advice with a compassionate approach. We support our clients to achieve a healthy lifestyle by decreasing risk factors for disease, normalizing lab values, and strengthening their relationship with food and body image.

WHO WE ARE:

Rebecca Bitzer & Associates (RBA) was founded by Rebecca Bitzer in 1989, which means we have been in the business of nutrition counseling for over 25 years! We got our start when Rebecca was rotating through physician offices seeing their clients. Since then, RBA has grown to two permanent office locations with multiple consultation rooms, seven Registered Dietitians, and an administrative staff of ten, making it the largest practice for food and nutrition-related care in the Maryland, Virginia, and the DC metropolitan area.

OUR PHILOSOPHY:

Our team of seven Registered Dietitians is truly passionate about what they do. They are grateful that every day they are sharing in their clients' journeys toward their nutrition and health goals. Our company culture places immense value on professional growth to be specialized in our individual areas of expertise. Additionally, RBA encourages our employees to prioritize personal self-care, to model the behavior for our clients. Our environment also encourages innovation, which means all ideas are listened to, no matter how small or grandiose. Our employees have the power to run with these ideas in order to create nutrition programs, improve customer service, or increase efficiency in the office. We are believers in empowering our employees by considering their strengths when assigning tasks and projects so they are able to succeed in what they are good at and find their place in our company. It is important to us that our employees come to work with a sense of pride, believing in themselves, our clients, and our company values.

Another facet of our company we are proud of is our mentorship track, which allows dietetic students to gain experience in private practice and work closely with our Registered Dietitians. With this coaching our nutrition interns are trained to become the next generation of Registered Dietitians, which we believe increases the value of our profession both in quality of nutrition care and business savvy. We have taken it upon ourselves to do our part in furthering the profession of nutrition and dietetics so that Registered Dietitians can do what they love and earn what they deserve!

LET RBA HELP YOU SUCCEED

For more inspiring tried and true information on how to be a REBEL RD, visit our website www.rbitzer.com

THERE YOU WILL LEARN HOW TO:

- **R** – Realize your potential
    - Obtain additional resources to supplement the reading and help you take the next step in your career.
- **E** – Excel in one area of dietetics
    - Align your personal and professional values.
    - Determine your VIP clients.
- **B** – Build your practice
    - Learn how to hire and pay employees.
    - Expand locations.
    - Create and fine-tune your systems.
- **E** – Empower your clients to be successful and happy
    - Get business coaching to help you develop your own successful program with resources and tracking information to help you measure success.
    - Learn how to become an insurance provider.
- **L** – Learn ways to keep your practice financially successful
    - Practice REBEL Success Strategies.
    - Utilize business coaching to help you set up your finances and budget.
- **R** – Reach new heights
    - Listen to audio and watch video clips from the book and other speaking engagements.
    - Read inspirational content to help you break out of your comfort zone.
- **D** – Dare to be a REBEL
    - Overcome your fears and take the next step to having the nutrition practice of your dreams.

SERVICES WE OFFER INCLUDE:

- Become a provider of medical insurance
- Bill your services to insurance
- Conquer the implementation of electronic health records
- Create innovative nutrition programs
- Formulate company policies and procedures
- Market your services to potential clients and influencers
- Become a leading force on social media
- Evaluate when you are ready and how to hire administrative staff or additional Registered Dietitian's to your practice

For even more nuts and bolts to assemble and run a successful private practice, we encourage you to sign up for our newsletter on www.rbitzer.com.

Made in the USA
San Bernardino, CA
08 September 2014